OTT-11
June, 1992

University and College Solid Waste Reduction and Recycling

by

Bruce A. Hegberg
Gary R. Brenniman
William H. Hallenbeck

University of Illinois Center for Solid Waste Management and Research

Office of Technology Transfer, Richard A. Wadden, Director
School of Public Health (M/C 922)
Box 6998
Chicago, Illinois 60680

© 1992 The Board of Trustees of The University of Illinois

Preface and Acknowledgments

This public service report is a result of the concern of the Illinois Governor, State Legislature, and the Public for the magnitude of the solid waste problem in Illinois. The concern led to the passage of the Illinois Solid Waste Management Act of 1986. One result of this Act was the creation of the University of Illinois Center for Solid Waste Management and Research. The Office of Technology Transfer (OTT) is part of this Center. One of OTT's means of transferring technology is the publication of public service reports which contain discussions of important topics in solid waste management.

Funding for this public service report was provided by the Illinois Department of Energy and Natural Resources (ENR), Office of Recycling and Waste Reduction. The views expressed in this report do not necessarily reflect the policy of the ENR. The authors would like to acknowledge the review provided by ENR and the valuable assistance of Mr. Tim Hoss, University of Illinois-Urbana Recycling Coordinator.

Copies of this report are available through the Office of Technology Transfer (M/C 922), School of Public Health, The University of Illinois at Chicago, Box 6998, Chicago, Illinois 60680, telephone 312-996-6927.

Disclaimer

Mention of company, trade names or commercial products does not signify endorsement or a recommendation of use by the University Center for Solid Waste Management and Research.

Summary

In 1990, the Illinois General Assembly enacted PA86-1363, a part of which is known as the "College Recycling Law." It requires each Illinois public university and community college to develop a comprehensive waste reduction plan covering an initial period of 10 years, followed by 5 year updates. Each plan is to be developed by January 1, 1995 and shall be designed to achieve by January 1, 2000 at least a 40% reduction in solid waste (from a base year of 1987) destined for landfill disposal.

The following manual is intended to assist those universities and colleges required to submit a waste plan to ENR. It is offered as a reference document which contains data pertinent to the subject law and also information concerning recycling and reduction activities. Other sources of information and data are available in the literature as well. A set of guidelines which details the format of plans, the topics to be addressed, and the procedures, rules and policies to be followed in accordance with the mandate are available from ENR.

The waste planning and reduction requirements of the College Recycling Law basically parallel similar requirements in Illinois and other states. Public colleges in California and New Jersey are required to develop mandatory recycling. Under the Solid Waste Planning and Recycling Act (PA85-1198 and PA86-228), Illinois counties are required to adopt and implement 20 year solid waste plans, which shall include recycling goals of 15% and 25% of municipal solid waste (MSW) by the end of the third and fifth years of implementation, respectively.

This report provides background data and recycling methodologies necessary to comply with the Illinois law. It provides universities and community colleges with guidance on how to address the elements of the College Recycling Law. Fifty community colleges and 12 universities (a total student population of approximately 250,000 full time and 300,000 part time students) are affected by the Illinois law. The plans must address/manage solid waste generated by academic, administrative, student housing and institutional functions.

Regardless of the type of waste reduction or recycling plan established as a result of the College Recycling Law, it is necessary to maintain a centrally managed recycling program and ensure visible support from the college administration. A centrally managed program will send clear messages to waste generators, thereby developing an increased response to recycling. Administration support is fundamental to promoting changes in the reduction and disposal of waste by students, staff, and faculty. Such support brings with it endorsement of the goals of a waste reduction/recycling program, financial backing, and a level of priority. It also forms the groundwork for long term waste handling policy changes and procurement procedure modifications.

Assessment of the campus solid waste stream and the waste of individual buildings is important for properly implementing recycling and in complying with the College Recycling Law. A waste stream assessment should provide the following information: (i) the rate at which waste is disposed and the sources (large and small) of waste; (ii) existing methods of waste disposal; (iii) components of the waste stream; (iv) recyclable components of the waste stream and their expected quantities; and (v) attitudes toward waste disposal and recycling. Three primary steps are necessary to determine the above information: an inventory of waste disposal on campus, a determination of waste generation quantities, and a waste characterization. Provided in the appendices are two procedures (Appendices B and C) and four forms (Appendix D) to assist in determining college specific waste generation quantities and waste characterization. This should provide sufficient data to make decisions about waste disposal for a college campus. A waste stream assessment should be conducted by one or more people, but for uniformity should be limited to a specific set of individuals. Members of the college recycling committee would be well suited, as they are obliged to be involved in modification of the waste stream. If the more generic (albeit less involved) college data presented in this report is used rather than the procedures provided in the appendices, accuracy with regard to waste and recyclable generation estimates, waste characterization, and waste and recyclables variability may be sacrificed.

Variation in waste stream quantities from colleges is largely due to the months in which a school is in session. The month of October is consistently high in generation, with little variability. Landscape waste generated during the fall season is the likely contributor. Another contributor is the start of the new academic year, when faculty and students are disposing of surplus materials generated around registration time. March and April exhibit a tendency to be above average, probably due to spring cleanup activities. Coincident with summer and winter break, disposal minima occur during either June, July, August, or December.

An average waste generation rate value for universities with campus housing is 820 lbs/student/year. Schools such as community colleges (which are primarily commuter schools) have generation rates which are much smaller, on the order of 180 lbs/student/year. This is likely due to decreased on-site living and a smaller staff. Even though listed as a per student value, these rates account for all on-campus waste generation. Limited per capita generation rate data for dining facility and dormitory settings have been measured at 0.36 lb/student/meal and 1.0 lb/student/day, respectively. There tends to be a reduction in waste generation per student as school size increases. For the range of student populations reviewed (1,100 - 41,000 students), $y = 1297.3 - 0.01976 \cdot x$, where y = campus waste generation on a per student basis (lb/student/year), and x = total number of enrolled students ($r^2 = 0.707$, n=14).

As may be expected, paper is the predominant component of college waste. It comprises an average 61% of the waste stream by weight, without adjustment of data for common components among schools. When reviewing mass basis waste characterization studies and excluding the highly variable component of landscape waste, the following average composition is determined:

Component	$\bar{x}$ (weight %)
Aluminum	2.3
Food Waste	8.6
Glass	5.7
Metal (non-aluminum)	2.6
Paper	
Corrugated	10.2
High grade office	15.0
Newsprint	10.7
Other paper	<u>29.9</u>
Paper Subtotal	65.8
Plastic	7.0
Wood Waste	3.2
Other	4.8
Total	100

Of all schools which were reviewed, paper consistently comprised nearly 2/3 of college waste streams, with little variability. Corrugated cardboard also shows little variability in comparison to other components. The average quantity of aluminum present (probably due to beverage cans) is higher than that found in 'typical' MSW (1.2% by weight). "Mixed paper," or not otherwise classifiable "other" paper consistently forms a predominant portion of the waste stream. If it is desired to recycle a majority of a college waste stream, it is necessary to identify methods to collect, separate, and market mixed and otherwise junk paper.

The portion of a waste component which can be recycled may vary widely from school to school. A waste sort should identify the proportion of waste components which are recyclable or not recyclable. For example, the aluminum content of the University of

British Columbia waste stream is 1.1% by weight, with 0.3% comprising foil food containers (which are difficult to recycle compared to aluminum beverage containers).

It should be noted that while corrugated cardboard comprises 5-10% of the waste stream by weight, it can occupy significantly more on a loose volume basis, and therefore greatly impact volumetric waste generation. Such material has comprised 25% and 75% of the University of Illinois-Urbana and Northwestern University waste stream sorts by volume, respectively.

Other components generally present in lesser amounts can include materials such as disposable diapers (0.3% by weight), aseptic packaging (0.1%) and fines (0.8%-4.25%). Textiles and special/hazardous wastes at three schools comprised 0.5-1.7% and 0.2-0.4% of the waste stream by weight, respectively.

Rates of college recycling from colleges with aggressive, nearly campus-wide recycling programs for the frequently collected materials of paper (office paper, newsprint) and corrugated cardboard are about 42 lbs/student/year and 19 lbs/student/year, respectively. Once again, these rates include the disposal on the parts of faculty, staff, and students.

There are three fundamental components of recycling: collection, processing, and marketing. Collection and/or processing are activities performed by a college staff or contractor. Two methods are typically used for waste collection and processing: i) collection of recyclables separated from the normal refuse stream at the source (termed source separation), followed by minimal processing (i.e., contaminant removal and subsequent material categorization); ii) collection of recyclables with the normal refuse stream followed by more extensive processing (mixed waste collection and recycling). For most colleges with recycling activities, source separation collection is used. The most commonly employed method is containerized collection at central locations inside and/or outside each building. Generators (office workers, faculty, housing residents) separate recyclable waste from refuse using recycling collection containers. In an office or desk setting, one container/sort is typically used. Dormitory and housing residents typically collect materials commingled and then perform a 2, 3, or 4 component sort upon emptying. Central collection containers are either emptied on-location with a refuse collection vehicle or interchanged with an empty container and transported to a processing facility. Processing includes additional sortation and removal of contaminants to an acceptable level, as well as densification for shipment to market.

Mixed waste collection in conjunction with centralized processing and removal of recyclables is a practice seldom utilized at colleges at this time. In fact, the only college program which includes such processing is at the University of California-Los Angeles.

The UCLA program is designed to be non-intrusive in nature. This can sacrifice generator education and awareness with regard to waste reduction and recycling (important elements of any recycling program). To perform an initial "selective" separation of mostly recyclable from mostly non-recyclable refuse, three separate collection routes, based on the general waste characteristics of each particular building, were established: i) commingled mixed paper and other recyclables, ii) standard refuse, and iii) landscape waste. Buildings whose refuse is predominantly paper are part of the mixed paper collection route (Route 1). Because all waste is processed, users of these buildings are not equipped with individual recycling containers and there is no in-building recycling. Buildings whose refuse may be questionable (i.e., potentially hazardous to process) or not easily recycled are part of the standard refuse (Route 2). Landscape waste routes are coordinated with area landscaping activities (Route 3). While mixed waste processing is the primary recycling method used, a limited amount of source separation is performed throughout the UCLA campus. Waste generating buildings which are on the refuse route (Route 2) who wish to be part of the recycling program are supplied with mixed paper route dumpsters upon request. Student housing facilities are serviced by all routes, and students perform source separation. Central collection containers are provided for commingled recyclables on each floor.

The College Recycling Law requires identification of frequently purchased products with recycled content and a policy dictum that recycled content materials be preferred over "virgin" content materials, assuming specifications are satisfied. Implicit in this is the necessary commitment that colleges will purchase products with recycled material content when such products are favorable in terms of conformance to specifications, cost, and availability.

A number of steps may be performed to encourage procurement of recycled content products. First, inventory the type and consumption rate of goods on-campus for which recycled content materials are available, and identify producers of such recycled content goods. Next, a cost analysis of purchasing virgin versus recycled products should be performed and weighed against normal purchasing requirements (i.e., conformance to specifications, availability, shipping, recycled content, and durability). Third, it is recommended that new products be tested by major campus users for acceptability. Fourth, the evaluation of a different pricing structure for recycled content versus virgin products should be investigated (e.g., a reduction in profit margin for recycled content products). A price preference to support the purchase of recycled content products may be possible. Lastly, a system to monitor the progress of recycled product procurement should be developed. Such monitoring should be included in annual recycling/waste management reports.

Table of Contents

Chapter   Page

1. Introduction 1
   1.1 Project Plan 6
   1.2 Administrative Support 9
   1.3 Forming a Program Team 9
       1.3.1 Recycling Committee 9
       1.3.2 Designating a Recycling Coordinator 10
2. Waste Stream Assessment 11
   2.1 Historical Waste Generation and Waste Generation Locations . . 13
   2.2 Inventory of Campus Waste Disposal 13
   2.3 Determination of Waste Generation 15
   2.4 Determination of Waste Characterization 16
   2.5 Determination of Recyclable Component Quantities 17
3. Waste Characterization and Generation Data 19
   3.1 Monthly Waste Stream Variation 19
   3.2 College Waste Stream Generation Rates 19
   3.3 College Waste Stream Compositions 22
       3.3.1 Campus Waste Stream 23
       3.3.2 Academic and Special Areas Waste Compositions . . 27
       3.3.3 Residential Areas Waste Compositions 31
   3.4 Monthly Recycling Stream Variation 31
   3.5 College Recycling Generation Rates 34
4. Buyers/Market Sources for Recyclables 37
   4.1 Finding the Right Recyclable Materials Dealers 37
   4.2 Dealers and Mill Consumers of Waste Paper 39
   4.3 Rural Area Markets 39
5. Strategies for Implementing College Waste Reduction 51
   5.1 Source Reduction 51
   5.2 Recycling 54
       5.2.1 Implementation Steps 55
       5.2.2 Model Department Recycling Policy 55
       5.2.3 Source Separation College Recycling 58
             5.2.3.1 Container Selection 58
             5.2.3.2 Container Site Selection 59
       5.2.4 Custodial Partnership 59
       5.2.5 Mixed Waste Collection College Recycling 60
   5.3 Processing of Recyclables 61
   5.4 Recycling Based on Facility Function 62
       5.4.1 Academic and Office Areas 62
       5.4.2 Housing and Residence Halls 62
       5.4.3 Food Service Waste Recycling 62
       5.4.4 Surplus Equipment and Scrap Recycling 64
       5.4.5 Chemical Redistribution 64
   5.5 Education and Promotion 65

Table of Contents

Chapter	Page
6. Recycling Implementation at Colleges	*67*
6.1 Cost Elements to Consider in College Recycling	*67*
6.2 Estimating College Recycling Costs	*68*
6.2.1 Actual Costs	*68*
6.2.2 Startup Cost Estimates	*68*
6.3 Exemplary College Recycling	*72*
6.3.1 Aggressive University Recycling Programs	*72*
6.3.2 Guidance Reports	*74*
7. Recycled Content Product Procurement	*75*
7.1 Procurement Policy Elements	*75*
7.2 Design for Recycling	*76*
7.3 Specifications for Recycled Content Products	*76*
7.4 Joint Purchasing	*78*
7.5 Sources of Recycled Content Products	*78*
Appendix A State of Illinois College Recycling Law (PA 86-1363)	*79*
Appendix B Procedure for Determination of Waste Generation from Limited Sample Sizes	*81*
Appendix C Procedure for Determination of Waste Characterization	*91*
Appendix D Waste Stream Assessment Forms	*105*
Form 1 Building Waste Assessment Form	*105*
Form 2 Waste Disposal Inventory Assessment Form	*106*
Form 3 Waste Composition Data Sheet	*107*
Form 4 Material Recycling Estimation Sheet	*108*
Appendix E Weight-Volume Conversions for Recyclables and Waste Components	*109*
Appendix F Illinois College Recycling Contacts	*111*
Appendix G Example Agreements for Marketing Recyclables	*119*
Exhibit G.1 Example Letter of Intent for Waste Paper Recycling	*119*
Exhibit G.2 Example Office Paper Collection Letter of Agreement	*120*
Exhibit G.3 Example Newspaper Recycling Contract	*122*
References	*125*

List of Tables

Table		Page
1.1	Publicly Supported Universities in Illinois	3
1.2	Publicly Supported Community Colleges in Illinois	4
3.1	Waste Generation Rates for College Settings	21
3.2	Waste Generation Rates for Institutional Settings	23
3.3	College Waste Compositions (Mass Basis)	24
3.4	College Waste Compositions (Volume Basis)	25
3.5	Average Composition of University Waste, Excluding Landscape Waste	27
3.6	Educational Areas Waste Compositions	28
3.7	Administrative Areas Waste Compositions	29
3.8	Specialty Areas Waste Compositions	30
3.9	Residential Areas Waste Compositions	32
3.10	Recyclable Generation Rates for College Settings	35
4.1	Markets for Waste Paper in Illinois and Neighboring States	40
4.2	Users of Newsprint for Manufacture of Cellulose Insulation	42
4.3	Waste Paper Dealers in Illinois and Surrounding States	43
5.1	Methods of Campus Waste Stream Reduction and Reuse	52
5.2	Materials Recycled at Colleges Based on Facility Type	54
5.3	Implementation Steps for Cornell University Recycling Program	56
6.1	Summary of Campus Recycling Costs	69
6.2	University of Illinois Five Year Recycling Implementation Budget	71
6.3	Aggressive University Recycling Programs	73
7.1	Recommended Minimum Recycled Content Standards for Paper and Paper Products	77
B.1	Quarter 1 Vehicle Tonnages from a Waste Collection Authority	89
B.2	Quarter 2 Vehicle Tonnages from a Waste Collection Authority	89
C.1	Typical Waste Component Categories	100
C.2	Description of Some Waste Component Categories	101
C.3	Values of Mean and of Standard Deviation (s) for Within Week Sampling to Determine College Waste Component Composition	102
C.4	Values of Mean and of Standard Deviation (s) for Within Week Sampling to Determine MSW Component Composition	102
C.5	Values of t Statistics (t*) as a Function of Number of Samples and Conference Interval	103

List of Tables (cont.)

Table *Page*

E.1	Waste and True Material Densities	109
E.2	Recyclable Materials	110
F.1	Recycling Activities and Waste Disposal/Recycling Contacts at Illinois Public Universities	111
F.2	Recycling Activities and Waste Disposal/Recycling Contacts at Illinois Public Community Colleges	113

List of Figures

Figure *Page*

1.1	Illinois Public Universities and Community Colleges	5
1.2	Precedence Diagram for College Recycling Law	7
2.1	Elements of a Waste Stream Assessment	12
2.2	College Campus Waste Stream Flow Paths	14
3.1	Monthly Variation in Municipal Waste Collection at the University of Michigan (Ann Arbor)	20
3.2	Monthly Variation in Municipal Waste Collection at George Washington University (Washington, D.C.)	20
3.3	Per Student College Waste Generation as a Function of School Size	22
3.4	Monthly Variation in Plastics, Old Corrugated Cardboard, and Food Waste in the Rutgers University Recycling Program	33
3.5	Monthly Variation in Mixed Paper, Glass and Cans in the Rutgers University Recycling Program	33
3.6	Monthly Variation of All Recyclables Collected at the University of Illinois-Urbana and Rutgers University	34
5.1	Cornell University Residence Hall Source Separation Arrangement	63

1. Introduction

In 1990, the Illinois General Assembly enacted PA86-1363, a part of which is known as the "College Recycling Law" (shown in Appendix A). It requires each Illinois public university and community college (collectively referred to in this report as "colleges") to develop a comprehensive waste reduction plan covering an initial period of 10 years, followed by 5 year updates. Each plan is to be developed by January 1, 1995 and shall be designed to achieve by January 1, 2000 at least a 40% reduction in solid waste (from a base year of 1987) destined for landfill disposal.

The following manual is intended to assist those colleges required to submit a waste plan to ENR. It is offered as a reference document which contains data pertinent to the subject law and also information concerning recycling and reduction activities. Other sources of information and data are available in the literature as well. A set of guidelines which details the format of plans, the topics to be addressed, and the procedures, rules and policies to be followed in accordance with the mandate are available from ENR.

The waste planning and reduction requirements of the College Recycling Law basically parallel similar requirements for Illinois counties established by the Solid Waste Planning and Recycling Act (Illinois Revised Statutes Ch. 85, ¶ 5953-5962). Under the Solid Waste Planning and Recycling Act, counties are required to adopt and implement 20 year solid waste plans. It also requires the plans to include goals of 15% and 25% recycling by the end of the third and fifth years of implementation, respectively.

Public colleges in other states are being required to comply with similar recycling requirements as well. Under the California Integrated Waste Management Act, schools which are part of the Cal State university system and the community college system are required to set goals of 25% and 50% recycling (by weight) by 1995 and 2000, respectively. Schools in the University of California system are not required to comply with the Act but are encouraged to participate. In accordance with the mandatory recycling law in New Jersey, all entities within a county (including universities and community colleges) are required to recycle a minimum number of specific components. The University of Minnesota Board of Regents passed a waste abatement policy which directed the administration to develop policies and plans to promote the separation of recyclables from university waste streams, develop specifications for increased use of recycled content/reusable products, and to develop an institutional materials waste reduction policy.

The purpose of this report is to provide background data and recycling methodologies necessary to comply with the Illinois law. It also provides universities and community colleges with guidance on how to address the elements of the College Recycling Law properly and in a thorough fashion. In all, 50 community colleges and 12 universities (Tables 1.1 and 1.2, Figure 1.1), with a total student population of approximately 250,000 full time and 300,000 part time students, are affected by the Illinois law. The solid waste plan from each community college and university is to address/manage solid waste generated by academic, administrative, student housing and institutional functions. Each plan needs to address the following elements shown below. Sections of this report which deal with an element are shown in parentheses:

i. Waste generation by volume (Chapter 2; Appendix B; Appendix D, Forms 1 and 2)

ii. Waste generation in base year 1987 (Chapter 2)

iii. Amount of waste subject to landfill disposal (Chapter 2; Appendix B; Chapter 3)

iv. Existing source reduction and recycling activities

v. Waste collection and disposal costs

vi. Waste stream composition (Appendix C; Chapter 3)

vii. Future waste management methods (Chapter 5)

viii. Identification of goals to reduce the amount of waste subject to landfill disposal (Chapter 5)

ix. Recycling of marketable materials, including white office paper, computer paper, corrugated cardboard, and landscape waste (Chapter 4)

x. Investigation of market potential for other recyclable materials in the waste stream (Appendix C; Forms 3 and 4; Chapter 4)

xi. Evaluation of procurement policies and practices to eliminate procedures which discriminate against recycled content products (Chapter 7)

xii. Evaluation of procurement policies and practices to identify products or items procured on a frequent or repetitive basis which may be substituted with recycled content products (Chapter 7)

xiii. Establishment of institutional policy to purchase products with recycled content whenever such products have met specifications and standards of equivalent products which do not contain recycled content (Chapter 7)

Table 1.1   Publicly Supported Universities in Illinois

			\multicolumn{3}{c}{1990 Student Data}		
School	Number [a]	Town	Full Time	Part Time	Total
Chicago State University	52	Chicago	3,035	4,117	7,152
Eastern Illinois University	1	Charleston	9,257	1,859	11,116
Governor's State University	9	University Park	814	4,781	5,595
Illinois State University	2	Normal	18,925	3,736	22,661
Northeastern Illinois University	53	Chicago	4,156	6,297	10,453
Northern Illinois University	3	DeKalb	17,458	7,051	24,509
Sangamon State University	4	Springfield	1,331	3,016	4,347
Southern Illinois University	5	Carbondale	19,081	5,003	24,084
Southern Illinois University	6	Edwardsville	7,037	4,649	11,686
University of Illinois at Chicago	54	Chicago	18,625	6,336	24,961
University of Illinois at Urbana	7	Urbana	32,539	5,624	38,163
Western Illinois University	8	Macomb	10,394	3,360	13,754
University Subtotal			142,652	55,829	198,481
Average Number Students			11,888	4,652	16,540

a. Shown in Figure 1.1.

Table 1.2 Publicly Supported Community Colleges in Illinois

School	Number [a]	Town	1990 Student Data Full Time	Part Time	Total
Belleville Area College	10	Belleville	3,391	10,789	14,180
Black Hawk College	11	Moline	2,498	4,081	6,579
City Colleges of Chicago					
City-Wide College	55	Chicago	1,400	8,204	9,604
Daley College (Richard J.)	56	Chicago	1,876	6,462	8,338
Kennedy-King College	58	Chicago	4,741	4,767	9,508
Malcom X College	59	Chicago	5,523	4,079	9,602
Olive-Harvey College	60	Chicago	4,025	4,738	8,763
Truman College (Harry S.)	61	Chicago	4,392	12,075	16,467
Washington College (Harold)	57	Chicago	1,639	6,674	8,313
Wright College (Wilbur)	62	Chicago	2,073	6,224	8,297
Danville Area Community College	13	Danville	1,410	2,124	3,534
Du Page, College of	14	Glen Ellyn	8,049	21,138	29,187
Elgin Community College	15	Elgin	1,805	5,261	7,066
Harper College (Wm. Rainey)	17	Palatine	4,485	12,024	16,509
Heartland Community College	18	Normal	n.a.	n.a.	n.a.
Highland Community College	19	Freeport	1,051	2,207	3,258
Illinois Central College	20	East Peoria	3,999	8,725	12,724
Illinois Eastern Community College					
Frontier Community College	16	Fairfield	221	2,166	2,387
Lincoln Trail College	32	Robinson	480	474	954
Olney Central College	26	Olney	820	786	1,606
Wabash Valley College	50	Mt. Carmel	720	2,889	3,609
Illinois Valley Community College	21	Oglesby	1,781	2,426	4,207
Joliet Junior College	24	Joliet	3,004	6,641	9,645
Kankakee Community College	25	Kankakee	1,013	2,776	3,789
Kaskaskia College	26	Centralia	1,496	1,773	3,269
Kishwaukee College	27	Malta	1,164	1,871	3,035
Lake County, College of	28	Grayslake	2,666	10,860	13,526
Lake Land College	29	Mattoon	1,953	2,484	4,437
Lewis and Clark Community College	30	Godfrey	1,728	4,158	5,886
Lincoln Land Community College	31	Springfield	2,076	5,641	7,717
Logan College (John A.)	22	Carterville	2,402	2,814	5,216
McHenry County College	33	Crystal Lake	798	2,970	3,768
Moraine Valley Community College	34	Palos Hills	4,595	9,006	13,601
Morton College	35	Cicero	878	3,317	4,195
Oakton Community College	36	Des Plaines	2,606	9,789	12,395
Parkland College	38	Champaign	3,283	5,287	8,570
Prarie State College	39	Chicago Heights	1,240	3,887	5,127
Rend Lake College	40	Ina	1,389	2,377	3,766
Richland Community College	41	Decatur	1,028	2,773	3,801
Rock Valley College	42	Rockford	2,317	6,413	8,730
Sandburg College (Carl)	12	Galesburg	944	1,695	2,639
Sauk Valley Community College	44	Dixon	1,123	1,986	3,109
Shawnee Community College	45	Ullin	818	757	1,575
Southeastern Illinois College	46	Harrisburg	1,286	1,746	3,032
South Suburban College of Cook County	43	South Holland	1,904	6,677	8,581
Spoon River College	47	Canton	757	1,213	1,970
State Community College	48	East St. Louis	607	629	1,236
Triton College	49	River Grove	5,199	11,560	16,759
Waubonsee Community College	51	Sugar Grove	1,357	4,732	6,089
Wood Community College (John)	23	Quincy	700	2,043	2,743
Community College Subtotal			106,710	246,188	352,898
Average Number Students			2,134	4,924	7,058

a. Shown in Figure 1.1.

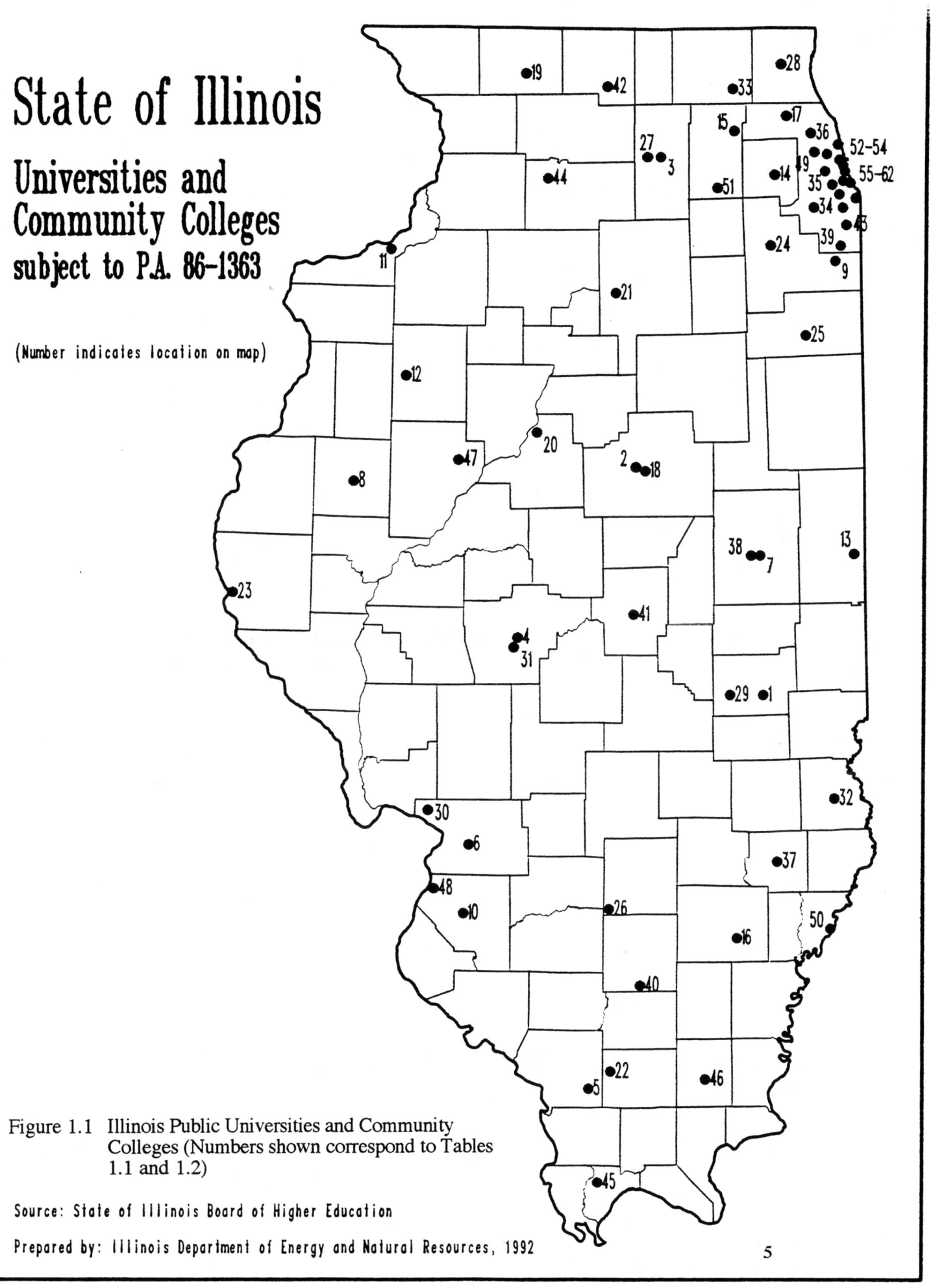

Figure 1.1 Illinois Public Universities and Community Colleges (Numbers shown correspond to Tables 1.1 and 1.2)

Source: State of Illinois Board of Higher Education

Prepared by: Illinois Department of Energy and Natural Resources, 1992

1.1 Project Plan

While elements i-xiii of the College Recycling Law are all related to college waste stream management, they may be summarized as three broader sets of project goals: assessment of past and current waste disposal practices (i - v), waste stream modification (vi - x), and procurement modification (xi - xiii). In order to coordinate the many individual sub-tasks necessary for compliance with the law, development of a work plan is recommended. The work plan will schedule individual tasks with regards to precedence, time duration and other related activities. A work plan is a simple ready reference document which can be used throughout a project to define what is to be done, when it is to be done, how much it will cost, how long it will take, and who will perform an activity. Depending on project complexity, a work plan may need to be nothing more than an action item list. In conjunction with the work plan, a task outline which consists of a brief summary of the scope of work required for fulfillment of a law (or a contract, if work is being contracted) should be developed. The following criteria can be used to evaluate the suitability of a task outline (Burstein 1990):

1. Does the task outline contain all of the deliverables required by the law ?
2. Can the same task outline be used to establish the project schedule ?
3. Can the same task outline be used to establish the project budget ?
4. Does each item listed meet criteria for inclusion in the task outline, i.e., scope, duration, and level of effort ?
5. Will the task outline require revision only if the law (or contract) is modified ?
6. Is the task outline general enough to accommodate routine changes in approach without being modified ?

If the answer to any of the above questions is "no," then more work is needed to finalize the task outline.

From the above work plan and task outline, the project schedule in terms of a precedence diagram can be developed.[1] A precedence diagram outlining the individual tasks of the three previously described project goals of the College Recycling Law is shown in Figure 1.2. This figure summarizes, on two pages, all of the actions which may be necessary to develop the solid waste plan and comply with the College Recycling Law. It is arranged with a project administration oversight schedule and three secondary schedules corresponding to the primary goals: past and current waste disposal practices, waste stream modification, and procurement modification. The flags A, B, C, D, E, F, G, and H serve to identify each primary goal and their interrelation. For example, before establishing a campus wide recycling program, an identification of current campus waste

---

[1] A concise discussion of the scheduling and budgeting methods as related to environmental engineering projects is shown in Burstein, 1990.

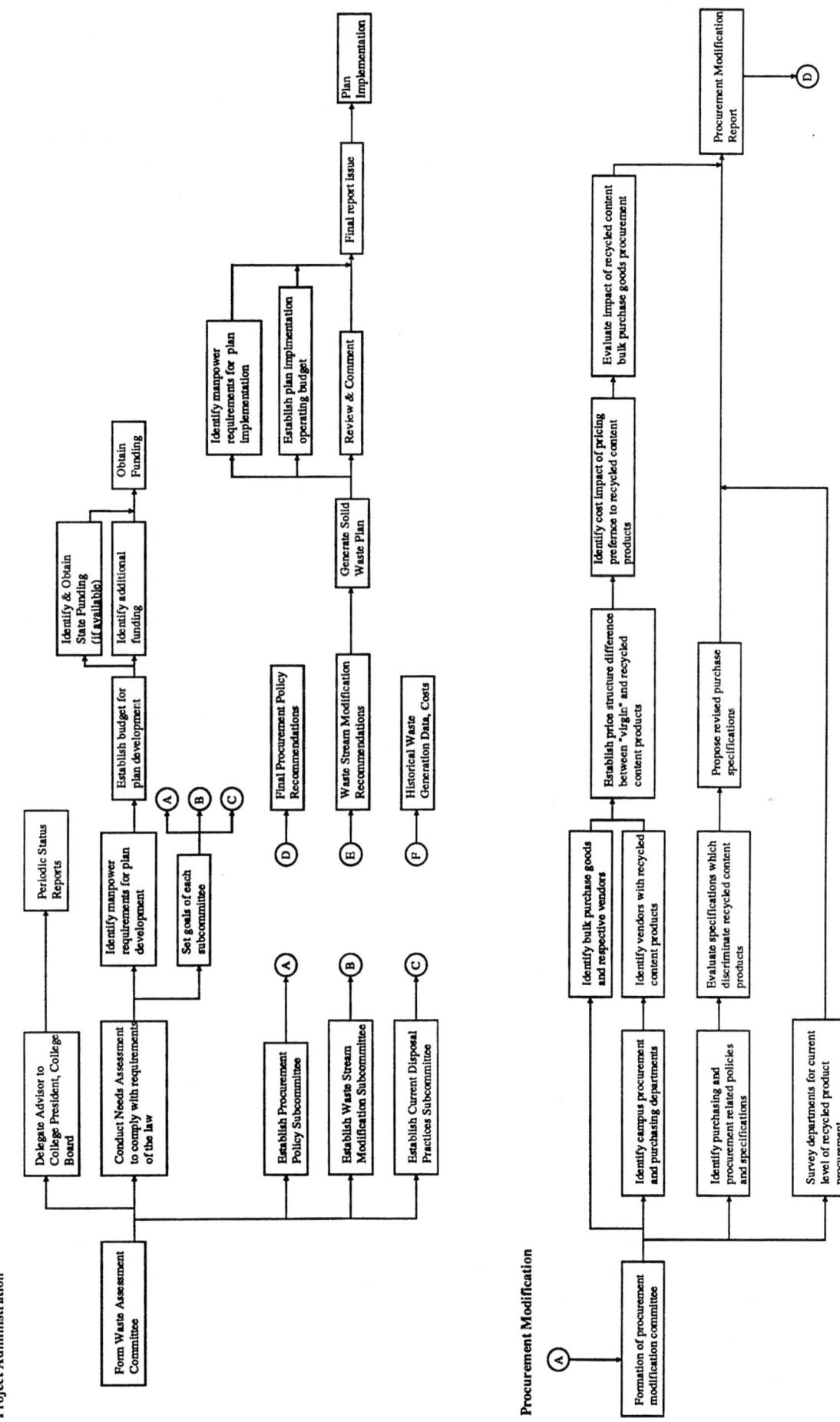

Figure 1.2 Precedence Diagram for College Recycling Law

Figure 1.2 (Cont.)

recycling activities and a departmental survey of independent activities should be conducted (flag H). As shown in the figure, most of the project goals can be completed independently of each other. The precedence diagram is a graphical representation of the solid waste plan tasks and the interactions among tasks. It identifies which tasks can be performed without dependence on others and where specific steps must be completed prior to proceeding. Usually, personnel assignments and project durations are also attached to each task. It is often chronological in nature.

1.2 Administrative Support

Regardless of the type waste reduction plan established as a result of the College Recycling Law, it is necessary to maintain a centrally managed recycling program and ensure visible support from the college administration. A centrally managed program will send clear messages to waste generators, thereby developing an increased response to recycling. Administration support is fundamental to promoting changes in the generation and disposal of waste by students, staff, and faculty. Such support brings with it endorsement of the goals of a waste reduction program, financial backing, and a level of priority. It also forms the groundwork for long term waste handling policy changes and procurement procedure modifications.

1.3 Forming a Recycling Committee

1.3.1 Recycling Committee

The formation of a recycling committee is an important first step in a campus waste reduction/recycling program. The committee should represent a cross-section of campus staff, faculty and students, including representatives from the following areas:

- Administration
- Business Affairs
- Custodial Staff
- Education
- Engineering
- Environmental Research
- Faculty
- Food Service
- Housekeeping
- Procurement/Purchasing
- Safety
- Student Government
- Waste Disposal / Physical Plant

1.3.2 Designating a Recycling Coordinator

One member of the recycling program team should be designated as the program coordinator. The recycling coordinator must evaluate progress toward completion of goals and resolve problems which arise. For universities, the position is usually full-time, while at community colleges it is part-time. The coordinator should be familiar with the campus facilities and waste disposal methods, be a good communicator, and address the day-to-day issues associated with recycling. Typical activities include campus educational programs, establishing work schedules for recycling activities, implementing strategies to reduce waste and reuse materials, improving recycling program effectiveness, working with recycled materials buyers/brokers, and working with university administrators and departments.

2. Waste Stream Assessment

Assessment of the campus solid waste stream and the waste of individual buildings is important for properly implementing recycling and in complying with the College Recycling Law. A waste stream assessment should provide the following information: (i) the rate at which waste is disposed and the sources (large and small) of waste; (ii) existing methods of waste disposal; (iii) components of the waste stream; (iv) recyclable components of the waste stream and their expected quantities; and (v) attitudes toward waste disposal and recycling. Three primary steps are necessary to determine the above information: an inventory of waste disposal on campus, a determination of waste generation quantities, and a waste characterization. This is shown diagrammatically in Figure 2.1. This should provide sufficient data to make decisions about waste disposal for a college campus.

Provided in the appendices are two procedures (Appendices B and C) and four forms (Appendix D) to assist in determining college specific waste generation quantities and waste characterization. Shown in Chapter 3 is accompanying data from other colleges across the country. It is not recommended that the more generic (albeit less involved) college data presented in Chapter 3 be used for planning purposes rather than the methods discussed in this chapter. Accuracy with regard to waste and recyclable generation estimates, waste characterization, and waste and recyclables variability will be sacrificed if average values are used. For example, a lack of proper determination may result in overestimation of waste generation, thereby requiring more to be recycled than stipulated by law. An improper waste characterization may not properly determine the portions of landscape waste or corrugated cardboard on campus, two components which are required to be diverted from landfill disposal.

Certain elements of the waste stream assessment described below may or may not already be well documented by a college administration. For example, the locations, quantities, and capacities of building dumpsters are no doubt well established; however, knowledge of specially handled waste from a building (such as solvents or used oil) may not be well known by the campus waste disposal staff. It is necessary to complete all portions of the waste stream assessment to obtain a complete picture.

A waste stream assessment should be conducted by one or more people, but for uniformity should be limited to a specific set of individuals. Members of the college recycling committee would be well suited, as they are obliged to be involved in modification of the waste stream.

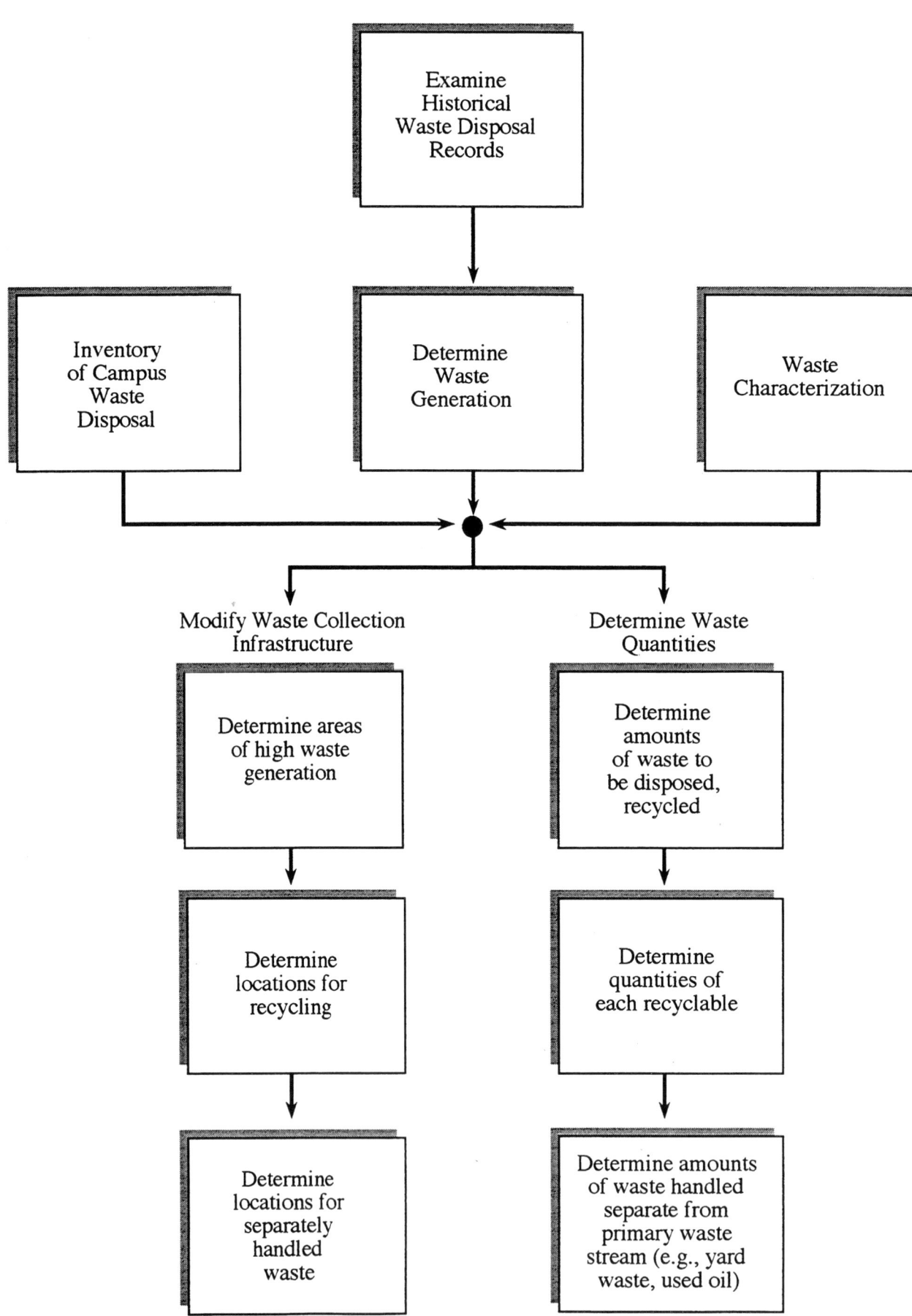

Figure 2.1   Elements of a Waste Stream Assessment

2.1 Historical Waste Generation and Waste Generation Locations

Since the base year of waste generation for the College Recycling Law is 1987, an estimate of past disposal amounts is necessary. If adequate disposal records do not exist for the 1987 year, contact the Illinois Department of Energy and Natural Resources for direction on estimating base year disposal quantities. The reason for choosing 1987 as the base year is largely due to the ensuing changes in Illinois solid waste legislation (i.e., landscape waste landfill ban, Solid Waste Planning and Recycling Act). In general, all historical data regarding college waste disposal should be identified.

Historical waste generation may be determined as follows, in order of preference:

- past disposal records (preferably quantitative tonnage data, however financial records may suffice)

- current estimates/records prorated to base year (using student population or disposal fees), while accounting for waste reduction, landscape waste diversion, and recycling

- per capita estimates of waste disposal

While past records which detail disposal quantities would be the most preferable method for determining historical generation, they can be difficult to locate and often do not contain sufficient detail.

Published per capita estimates of waste disposal, although the easiest to use for determining waste generation, may not be accurate and therefore are the least desirable for establishing historical campus disposal quantities. As is shown in Chapter 3, there is significant variation which exists among school waste generation rates (Table 3.1, p. 21). Additionally, the function of a campus has a large impact on waste disposal quantities (e.g., commuter vs. residence campus, 2 year vs. 4 year school, presence of a hospital or sports facility). However, a per capita estimate may be used to provide a comparison of what is measured against waste generation based on school size (Figure 3.3, p. 22).

2.2 Inventory of Campus Waste Disposal

A campus waste disposal inventory is one simple method to identify the waste disposal routes within each building and around campus. The waste disposal inventory allows documentation of each area's waste generating processes and operations, and provides a relative indication of large and small waste generators. All waste-generating aspects of a campus should be identified when conducting the inventory (Figure 2.2). A campus waste disposal inventory should include the following tasks:

- Establish a common assessment format for each building/waste stream

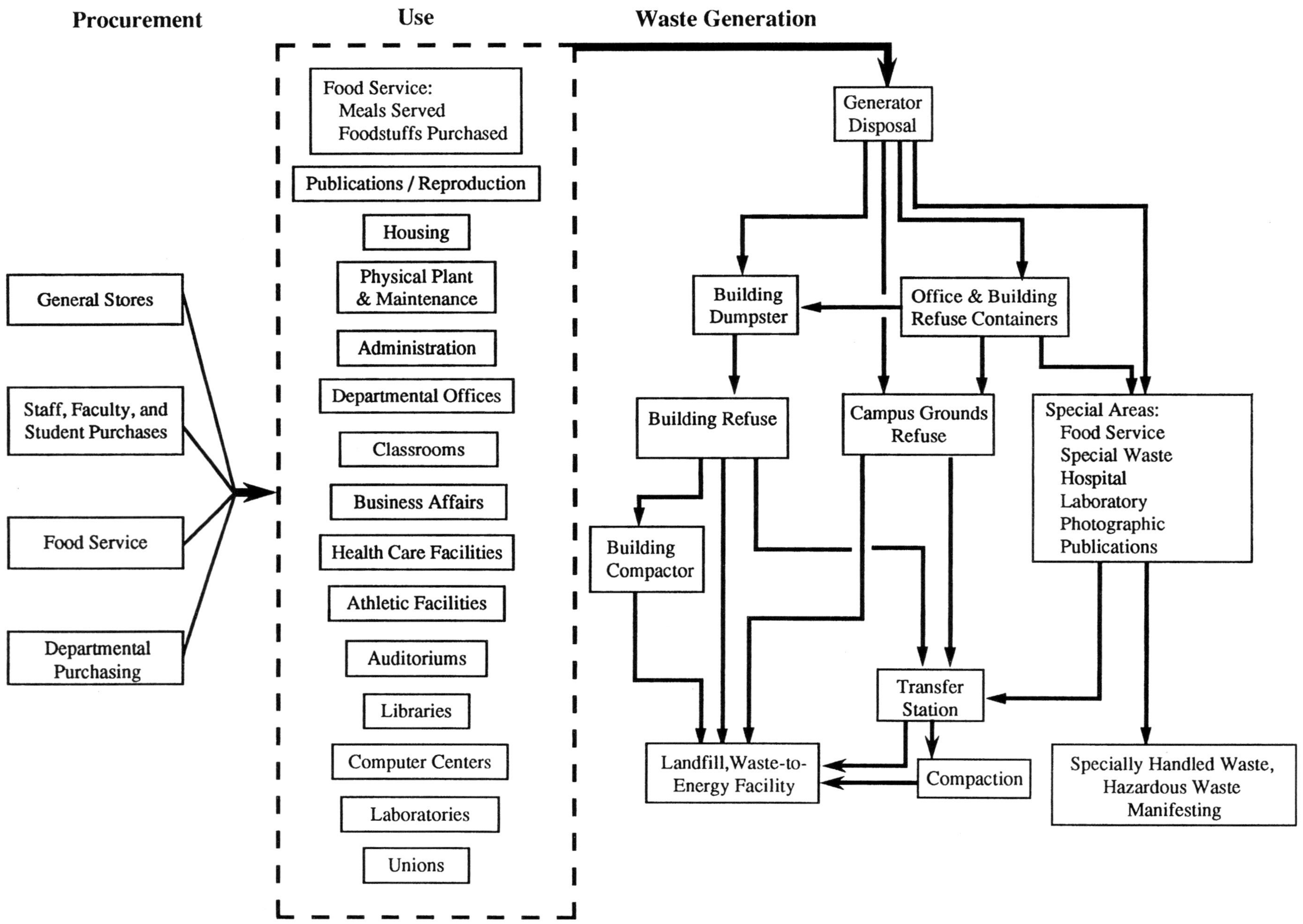

Figure 2.2 College Campus Waste Stream Flow Paths (without recycling)

- Identify the primary function(s) of a building

- Conduct multiple walkthroughs during normal business/school hours to observe actions

- Prepare a <u>preliminary</u> estimate of composition and quantity of waste disposed based on visual observation, and discussion with building personnel and janitorial staff

- Document abnormalities in refuse disposal (e.g., periodic excessive amounts) and oversizing/undersizing of building refuse dumpsters based on discussions regarding waste disposal with building residents and janitorial staff

- Follow the life cycle of materials, from when they enter a building to when they become waste products in a refuse container

Forms 1 and 2 are provided in Appendix D at the end of this report to assist in conducting the inventory. Although Form 2 (courtesy U.S. Postal Service, 1991) contains information regarding total number of cubic yards generated from each building surveyed, it is intended to be used as a relative indication of generator size. A method of accurately determining generation rates on campuses using limited sample sizes is provided in section 2.3. Attention should be paid to examining waste quantities present in building dumpsters (Form 2) prior to a waste pull (container emptying). This indicates potential sites where frequency of collection/dumpster size may be downgraded in conjunction with recycling. Forms 1 and 2 should identify: large and small waste generators on campus; what locations are appropriate targets for recycling; and areas where unique waste must be handled separate from the typical municipal solid waste stream.

2.3 Determination of Waste Generation

The quantity of waste generated on campus may be determined using the following methods:

- volume/tonnage records of haulers, landfill operators, recyclers or campus staff which continuously record waste quantities as a matter of policy/contract obligation

- waste measurements using limited weighings

- per capita estimates of waste disposal

While estimating volume/tonnage utilizing existing records of haulers, landfill operators, recyclers or campus staff appears as an obvious method, there are a number of associated problems. First, haulers generally charge for building waste disposal on a per stop basis, regardless of the waste quantity within a dumpster. This can provide an extremely high estimate of campus waste generation. Second, campus staff or haulers rarely record waste quantities present in dumpsters (% full), which is the reason for the waste disposal inventory in Section 2.2. Third, landfills generally charge on a volume basis (by the compacted truckload), and therefore the actual quantity of weight or original volume generated is unknown. Fourth, only fees for waste disposal are often recorded, with no indication of price per unit volume/mass. Fifth, college campuses seldom posses a truck scale for weighing quantities generated. Sixth, haulers which are contracted for campus waste disposal may understandably stop at other businesses before or after campus refuse pickup.

Unless refuse quantities are continuously weighed using criteria which avoids the above stated problems, the most economical and accurate method for determining refuse generation is using limited weighings. Tonnage estimation using limited weighings is straightforward to use, requires the minimum of effort to collect data, and is adaptable to waste management operations of varying complexity (Rushbrook and Ball, 1988). The number of weighings are determined based on the statistical confidence desired and the maximum allowable error. The suggested procedure for determining the waste generation from limited samples, based on Rushbrook and Ball, is shown in Appendix B at the end of this report. It requires temporary use of a truck scale for weighing differing refuse collection vehicles, e.g., roll-off type refuse containers, rear load packers, building dumpsters, or lugger boxes. This method is also suitable for tracking on a personal computer.

Per capita estimates of waste disposal, especially for educational settings, are poorly documented and have high variability. They will therefore provide inaccurate generation estimates.

2.4 Determination of Waste Characterization

The composition of solid waste from community colleges and universities is different from that of typical municipal solid waste. For example, quantities of paper are significantly higher. Unfortunately, there is little college waste stream composition data available, and of the data which is available, there is significant variability. Additionally, the waste stream components and/or sampling methodologies for the college waste characterizations are seldom similar. Data and examples of available university waste characterizations are shown in Chapter 3.

A college waste characterization may be performed on a per building basis or en masse. While examining waste on a per building basis may be useful in targeting recycling quantities from specific areas, accurate waste characterizations from each type of building would require significant expense and time. It is therefore recommended that an aggregate waste characterization be performed.

There are two methods for determining aggregate waste compositions: truckload sampling and spot sampling. Truckload sampling consists of sorting large (3-4 ton) MSW loads on approximately 5 separate occasions for statistical accuracy. In using spot sampling, literature has shown that waste compositions using sample sizes as small as 200-300 lb are statistically acceptable (Carruth and Klee, 1969). This has since become the minimum amount characterized for use in spot sampling. The "cone-and-quarter" technique has traditionally been used for obtaining representative spot samples: mix into an inverted cone shape an amount of waste which is at least four times the desired sample size, quarter the pile, and then remove one-quarter for analysis. Only one random sample should be taken from a refuse container/truck.

Shown in Appendix C is the suggested procedure for determining waste characterization. It is adapted from a draft method developed by American Society for Testing and Materials (ASTM) committee D34.01.02-Waste Sampling. The procedure requires a minimum number of samples (different from the minimum number of samples above for waste generation) based on the statistical confidence and precision desired. In general, 20 samples should be expected to be taken. Form 3 is provided in Appendix D to assist in logging characterization data, and calculating the volume % and weight % of the waste components (courtesy ASTM, 1991; U.S. Postal Service, 1991). To perform a weight to volume conversion, an appropriate density (based on the type of waste and its compactness) must be chosen. Appendix E shows typical conversion values for refuse, yard waste and recyclables.

It should be noted that care should be taken in performing the actual waste sort. Municipal waste can contain a variety of unsafe materials. It should not be unusual to expect such items as needles, broken glass, acids, liquid and solid chemicals, and animal carcasses. Appropriate personnel protection should be established and safety guidelines developed prior to sorting.

If a waste stream characterization is determined to be too involved an effort, limited college waste data is shown in Chapter 3. However, this data could be quite different from the waste stream of a specific Illinois college.

2.5 Determination of Recyclable Component Quantities

To assist in targeting the recovery amounts of waste stream recyclables, Form 4 in Appendix D is provided (courtesy U.S. Postal Service, 1991). The total quantities of components in municipal waste generated on campus (recyclable or otherwise) are identified after the waste generation and waste composition is determined. When combined with the collection amounts of components already being recycled, the total generation of a component can be determined. Estimated recovery efficiencies from the waste stream (termed the capture efficiency) can then be used to target the recovery rate of a recyclable.

3. Waste Characterization and Generation Data

Waste stream characterization and generation rate studies, as discussed in Chapter 2, supply data which becomes the basis for planning, designing and managing a waste stream handling system. This chapter summarizes data of college waste streams for the purposes of providing comparison and a general expectation of monthly variations, generation rates, waste stream content, recycling stream compositions, and recycling quantities.

3.1 Monthly Waste Stream Variation

Variation in waste stream quantities from colleges is largely due to the months in which a school is in session. Shown in Figures 3.1 and 3.2 respectively, are the monthly amounts of waste generated for the University of Michigan-Ann Arbor over a 4 year period and the monthly amounts of waste generated at George Washington University over a 3.5 year period. The charts show monthly average and high/low range based on percentages of the annual total. Because the monthly quantities shown are based on percent of annual total, year-to-year decreases (e.g., waste reduction, recycling) or increases in waste are factored out. The effect of landscape waste is included in the figures. For both schools, the month of October is consistently high, with little variability. Landscape waste generated during fall is the likely contributor. It has also been suggested that October is a maximum because students and faculty are just settling down after the start of the new academic year, and are disposing of the surplus materials generated around registration time (Chiu, et. al., 1976). March and April exhibit a tendency to be above average, no doubt due to students and campus grounds spring cleanup. Coincident with summer and winter break, the figures show disposal minima during either June, July, August, or December.

3.2 College Waste Stream Generation Rates

Waste stream generation rates from various universities/functions are shown in Table 3.1. The rates shown generally do not include yard waste nor construction debris. An average waste generation rate value for universities with campus housing is 820 lb/student/year. Even though listed as a per student value, this rate accounts for all on-campus waste generation. Since this value embodies the student, staff and faculty populations, the waste generated is significantly less than the national average MSW generation rate of 1500 lb/person/year (USEPA, 1990a). Therefore, using the per capita

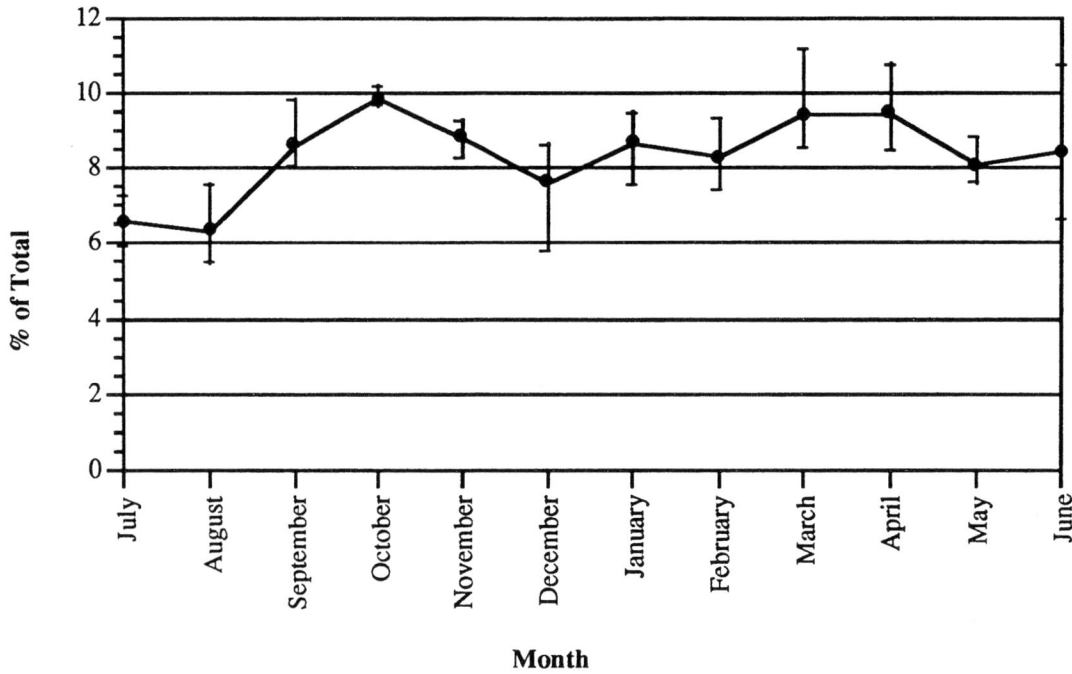

Figure 3.1　Monthly Variation in Municipal Waste Collection at the University of Michigan (Ann Arbor) as a Percentage of Annual Total. Four year average (FY 87 - FY 90) with high/low range shown. Data from Marks, 1991.

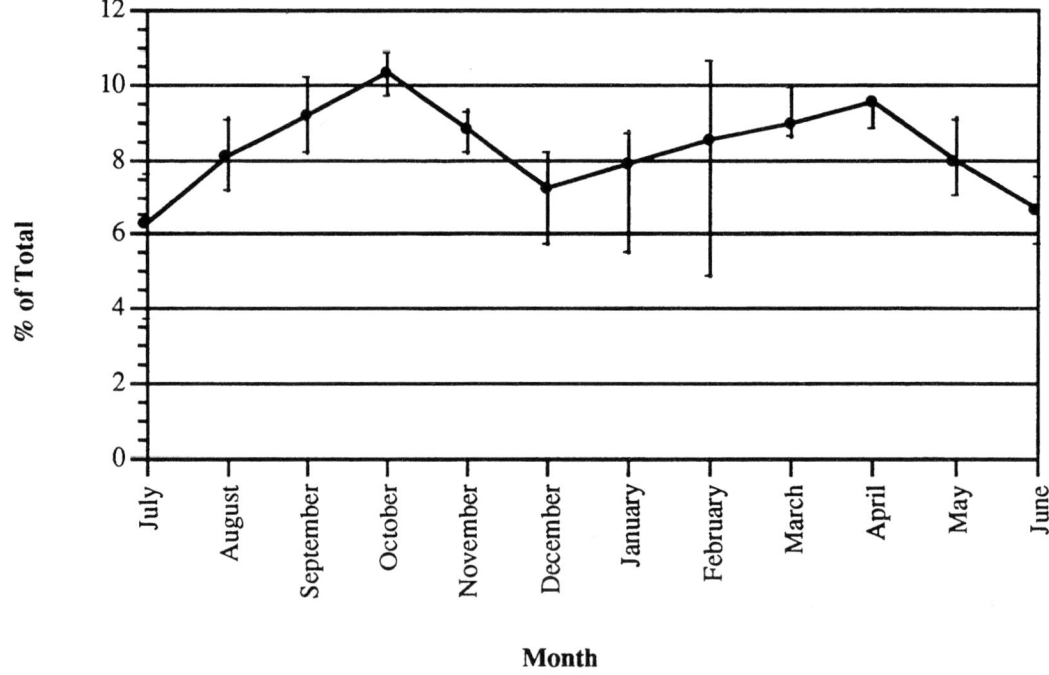

Figure 3.2　Monthly Variation in Municipal Waste Collection at George Washington University (Washington, D.C.) as a Percentage of Annual Total. Three and one-half year average (1972 - June 1975) with high/low range shown. Data from Chiu, et al, 1976.

Table 3.1   Waste Generation Rates for College Settings [a]

Generator Type	Unit Waste Factor		Source of Data
Universities with student housing [b] (combined areas waste stream)			
Concordia College	1200	lb/student/year	Becker, et. al., 1988
Cornell University	980	lb/student/year	Smithers, 1991
Dartmouth University	1080	lb/student/year	Skomra, 1989
University of Illinois-UC	840	lb/student/year	Hoss, 1991
University of Illinois-Chicago	1100	lb/student/year	Getz, 1990
University of Iowa	580	lb/student/year	Casey, 1991
Northwestern University	1280	lb/student/year	NU, 1990
North Carolina State University	680	lb/student/year	Franks, 1991
University of Michigan	730	lb/student/year	Marks, 1990
University of Minnesota	450	lb/student/year	UM, 1990
Rutgers	500	lb/student/year	Ching, 1991
Texas A&M	380	lb/student/year	Potter, 1990
Yale University	1200	lb/student/year	May, 1989
University British Columbia	490	lb/student/year	UBC, 1991
Average	820	lb/student/year	
Commuter colleges (primarily without student housing) [b]			
Triton College	200	lb/student/year	Becker, et. al., 1988
Univ. Wisconsin-Parkside	135	lb/student/year	UWP, 1990
Washtenaw Co., Mi.	220	lb/student/year	Glysson, 1990
Average	185	lb/student/year	
Residence Hall/Dormitory Waste			
Cornell University [c]	1.0	lb/student/day	Smithers, 1991
Dining Hall/Food Service Waste			
Cornell University [c]	0.36	lb/person/meal	Smithers, 1991

a. Including recyclables.
b. Quantities shown represent all waste generated in a college setting: food service, academic, dormitory waste, office waste, and other waste on a per student basis. The per student values shown include waste generated by staff and faculty as well. The values shown also include break periods (school year of approximately 255 days).
c. When in session.

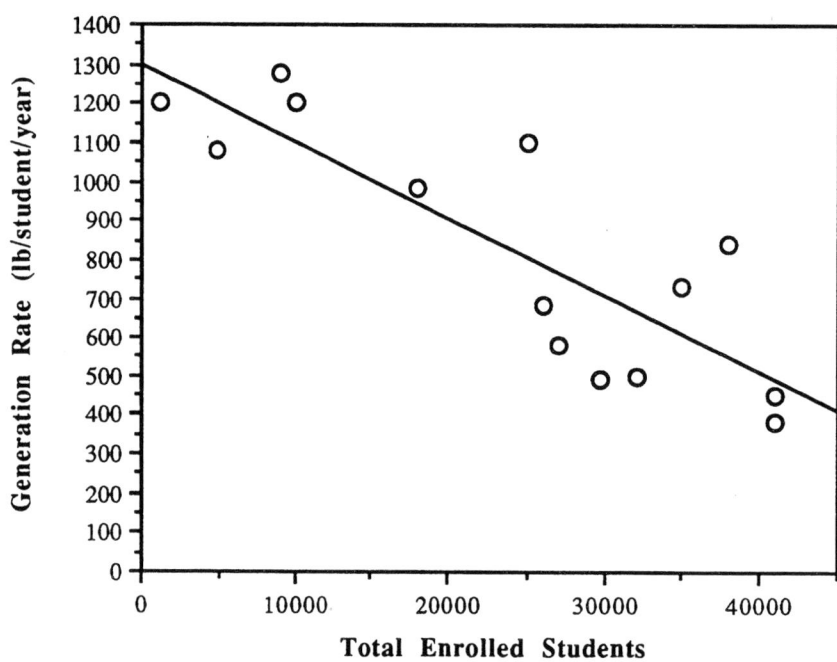

Figure 3.3 Per Student College Waste Generation as a Function of School Size. For the range of student populations reviewed (1100 - 41,000), y = 1297.3 - 0.01976 · x, where y = Campus waste generation on a per student basis (lb/student/year), and x = Total number enrolled students (r^2 = 0.707, n=14).

national average would significantly overestimate on-campus waste generation. Table 3.1 also shows limited per capita generation rates for dining facility and dormitory settings as measured at Cornell University. There tends to be an economy of scale with regards to school size: Cornell, Illinois, Michigan, Minnesota, N.C. State, Rutgers, and Texas A&M (all large schools) have a lower per student generation rate than Concordia, Cornell, Dartmouth, and Northwestern (smaller schools). This is shown graphically in Figure 3.3. Schools such as community colleges which are primarily commuter schools have generation rates which are much smaller, on the order of 180 lb/student/year (Table 3.1). This is likely due to decreased on-site living and a smaller employment staff. Additionally, shown in Table 3.2 are waste generation rates for types of generators similar to that which may arise in a college setting.

3.3 College Waste Stream Compositions

Shown in the following subsections are waste stream compositions from varying colleges and college functions. There are few colleges which have coordinated the efforts necessary for a waste sort. It should be noted that the number of samples or sample sizes for some of the waste sorts shown are inadequate, and detailed conclusions with regard to

Table 3.2   Waste Generation Rates for Institutional Settings

Generator Type	Waste Generation Rate		Source of Data
Hospitals	4.5	lb/staff/day	Glysson, 1990
	31.5	lb/bed/day	Becker et al., 1990
	0.2	yd^3/occupied bed/day	BFI, 1987
Patient Care	8.6	lb/bed/day	Glysson, 1990
Hospital Food Service	2.7	lb/bed/day	Glysson, 1990
Rehabilitation Care	6.4	lb/bed/day	Glysson, 1990
Commercial Buildings			
Office Buildings	1.5	lb/employee/day	Glysson, 1990
Offices	1	yd^3/10,000 ft^2/day	BFI, 1987
Department Stores	1	yd^3/2500 ft^2/day	BFI, 1987
Supermarkets	1	yd^3/1250 ft^2/day	BFI, 1987
Multiple Housing Unit	2.7	lb/resident/day	Glysson, 1990
Singles or no children	1.25	yd^3/unit/month	BFI, 1987
Family	1.75	yd^3/unit/month	BFI, 1987
Hotels/Motels, High Occupancy	0.5	yd^3/room/week	BFI, 1987
Hotels/Motels, Average Occupancy	0.2	yd^3/room/week	BFI, 1987

specific waste stream components at specific schools should not be made. When viewed as a group although, the waste compositions shown are believed to reflect that of a typical college. Unfortunately because of the number of samples required for a thorough waste sort, a professionally contracted waste sort is costly. However, inadequate sampling frequencies/sample sizes result in unrepresentative waste compositions. As a minimum, the college compositions shown will illustrate a general average for primary components and variability which can be expected due to daily activities, location, and procurement practices.

3.3.1 Campus Waste Stream

Waste stream compositions from a number of colleges are shown in Table 3.3 (weight basis) and Table 3.4 (volume basis). When available, the quantity of waste sampled is shown. Since volumetric measurements are subject to large fluctuations in density, primary emphasis should be given to Table 3.3.

As may be expected, paper is the predominant component of college waste, comprising an average 61% of the waste stream by weight, without adjustment of the data for common components among schools in Table 3.3. Paper composition at one university (not shown in Table 3.3) has been estimated as high as 75% by weight (Potter, 1990).

Table 3.3 College Waste Compositions (Mass Basis) [a]

Component	UCLA (Weight %)	Univ. Washington at Seattle (Weight %)	Northwestern University (Weight %)	University Cal. at Berkley (Weight %)	Dartmouth College (Weight %)	University of British Columbia (Weight %)	Yale University (Weight %)
Aluminum	3.7	1.0	3.8	0.7	3.0	1.1	b
Food	-	3.7	15.9	1.9	10.9	8.0	-
Glass	-	4.0	5.2	1.9	10.0	3.7	7.0
Landscape Waste	1.8	0.5	-	17.7	6.3[c]	15.9	6.0[c]
Metals (not inc. aluminum)	3.5	5.7	0.5	2.2	0.8	2.6	2.0
Paper							
Colored Paper	-	d	2.1	-	3.1	d	d
High Grade Office Paper	-	6.1	16.0	18.2	10.0	22.4	8.0
Mixed Paper	-	20.5	d	15.2	d	d	d
Other Paper [e]	-	21.4	26.2	6.8	29.6	15.0	18.0
Old Corrugated Cardboard	-	10.9	8.2	9.8	4.7	8.7	14.0
Old Magazines	-	d	-	2.6	d	d	6.0
Old Newsprint	-	5.6	14.3	7.9	11.4	4.4	16.0
Paper Subtotal	65.5	64.5	66.8	60.6	58.8	50.4	62.0
Plastic							
Film	-	-	-	2.6	3.9	-	-
PS Foam	-	0.6	1.0	0.6	1.0	-	-
HDPE	-	0.05	1.0	0.1	0.1	0.2	-
PET	-	0.04	f	0.0	0.8	5.5[g]	-
Other Plastic	-	6.8	1.8	2.1	3.5	3.3	-
Plastic Subtotal	1.9	7.5	3.8	5.4	9.4	9.0	8.0
Wood	3.5	4.6	-	0.7	-	3.0	3.0
Other [h]	22.0	8.5	4.0	8.9	0.9	6.3	12.0
Total	100	100	100	100	100	100	100
Toal Quantity Weighed (lbs.)	-	45,000	490	-	2,148,000	-	-
Source of Data	UCLA, 1991	UW, 1989	NU, 1990	Savage, 1991	DC, 1988	UBC, 1991	May, 1989

a. Aggregate composition for all university waste shown.
b. Included as part of metals.
c. Includes other organics (e.g., wood, textiles, dirt, cat litter).
d. Included as part of "Other Paper."
e. Includes paper which may / may not be recyclable (e.g., windowed envelopes, magazines, tissue, toweling, composite paper packaging).
f. PET amount included with HDPE.
g. Includes other container plastics.
h. "Other" includes items such as ash, non-classifiable organics and inorganics, special waste, diapers, batteries, inert solids, textiles, leather, etc.

Table 3.4 College Waste Compositions (Volume Basis) [a]

School	University of Illinois (Volume %) Loose	Geo. Washington University (Volume %) Loose	Northwestern University (Volume %) Loose	Dartmouth College (Volume %) Compacted	Yale University (Volume %) Loose
Aluminum	2.0	-	1.5	7.1	[b]
Food	-	2.3	1.8	2.6	-
Glass	2.0	-	0.6	3.6	3.0
Landscape Waste	8.5	-	-	1.7	2.0[c]
Metals (not inc. aluminum)	2.0	6.6	0.3	0.5	2.0
Paper					
Colored Paper	-	-	1.0	4.1	-
High Grade Office Paper	15.0	-	7.5	8.2	7.0
Other Paper [d]	25.0	-	5.1	38.6	23.0
Old Corrugated Cardboard	25	-	74.6	10.9	27.0
Old Magazines	-	-	-	-	3.0
Old Newsprint	2.0	-	2.7	7.2	5.0
Paper Subtotal	67.0	76.7	91.0	68.9	65.0
Plastic					
Film	-	-	-	-	-
PS Foam	-	-	1.3	6.2	-
HDPE	-	-	0.6	0.0	-
PET	-	-	e	0.4	-
Other Plastic	-	5.3	1.2	8.5	-
Plastic Subtotal	7.0	5.3	3.1	15.1	18.0
Wood	-	-	-	-	2.0
Other	11.5 [f]	9.1	1.7	0.5	9.0
Total	100	100	100	100	100
Source of Data	UIUC, 1988	Chiu et. al., 1976	NU, 1990	DC, 1988	May, 1989

a. Aggregate composition for all university waste shown.
b. Included as part of metals.
c. Includes other organics (e.g., wood, textiles, dirt, cat litter).
d. Including other paper which may / may not be recyclable (e.g., windowed envelopes, magazines, tissue, toweling, composite paper packaging).
e. PET amount included with HDPE.
f. Includes food waste.

Throughout the tables which follow "mixed paper," or not otherwise classifiable "other" paper forms a predominant portion of the waste stream. If it is desired to recycle a majority of a college waste stream, it is necessary to identify methods to collect, separate, and market mixed and otherwise junk paper.

Note the proportion by weight of waste stream components which are typically included in a recycling program in a college setting (Table 3.3): aluminum (0.7-3.8%), high grade office paper (typically white, 10.0-18.2%), old corrugated cardboard (OCC, 4.7-9.8%), old newsprint (ONP, 4.4-14.3%), colored paper (2.1-3.1%), landscape waste (1.8-17.7%), metals (0.5-6.8%), and plastics (1.9-9.4%).

When comparing data among schools, care should be taken to adjust for primary components which may not have been counted. For example, Northwestern University did not account for landscape waste. Since waste in Illinois is to expected to exclude landscape waste, and this parameter varies significantly due to school setting, it makes sense to exclude the landscape waste parameter altogether in the comparison of university waste streams (Landscape waste diversion can of course be counted toward Illinois waste reduction goals). This makes the averages determined a more reliable number to compare among schools. After adjusting data shown in Table 3.3 to exclude landscape waste, average constituents of university waste by weight are as shown in Table 3.5. From this data, a number of conclusions can be drawn. As expected, paper consistently comprises nearly 2/3 of college waste streams, with little variability. Corrugated cardboard also shows little variability in comparison to the other components. The average quantity of aluminum present (probably due to beverage cans) is higher than that found in 'typical' MSW (1.2% by weight). These results were used for Table C.3 of Procedure C to form the base composition required for determining the minimum number of samples necessary to perform waste sorts for college waste.

The portion of a waste component which can be recycled may vary widely from school to school. A waste sort should identify the proportion of each waste component which is recyclable or not recyclable. For example, the proportion of recyclable glass (e.g., container glass) as well as non-recyclable glass (e.g., window glass, light bulbs) should be determined. The aluminum content of University of British Columbia (UBC) waste stream is 1.1% by weight (Table 3.3), and of this 0.3% is foil food containers, which are difficult to recycle compared to aluminum beverage containers. The Dartmouth College waste sort identified aluminum as 3% by weight of the waste stream, with beverage containers comprising 2.76% and other forms of aluminum 0.24% (Dartmouth College, 1988). The UBC waste stream additionally contains 3.7% glass by weight, of

Table 3.5 Average Composition of University Waste, Excluding Landscape Waste [a]

Component	No. Schools [b] (n)	$\bar{x}$ (weight %)	s (weight %)	CV ($s/\bar{x}$)
Aluminum	6	2.3	1.4	0.61
Food Waste	5	8.6	5.6	0.65
Glass	6	5.7	3.0	0.53
Metal (non-aluminum)	7	2.6	1.8	0.69
Paper				
Corrugated	6	10.2	3.4	0.33
High grade office	6	15.0	8.1	0.54
Newsprint	6	10.7	4.7	0.44
Other paper	-	29.9	-	-
Paper Subtotal	7	65.8	4.2	0.06
Plastic	7	7.0	3.2	0.45
Wood Waste	5	3.2	1.4	0.44
Other	-	4.8	-	-

a. Summarized from the studies shown in Table 3.4. 'Other' and 'Other paper' determined by default.
b Number (n) determined from schools in Table 3.3 which measured the component listed.

which only 2.2% was potentially recyclable. Of 4.0% by weight glass at the University of Washington (UW), only 0.08% was non-recyclable.

It should be noted that while OCC comprises 5-10% of the waste stream by weight, it can occupy significantly more on a loose volume basis, and therefore greatly impacts volumetric waste generation. As shown in Table 3.4, OCC comprises 25% and 75% of the University of Illinois-Urbana and Northwestern University waste stream sorts by volume, respectively.

Other components generally present in lesser amounts (and therefore classified as 'Other') can include materials such as disposable diapers (0.3% by weight), aseptic packaging (0.1%) and fines (0.8%-4.25%), as measured at UBC and UW. Textiles at three schools comprised 0.5-1.7% of the waste stream by weight (Savage, 1991; UBC, 1991; UW, 1989). Special/hazardous wastes at three schools comprised 0.2-0.4% of the waste stream by weight (Savage, 1991; UBC, 1991; UW, 1989).

3.3.2 Academic and Special Areas Waste Compositions

Waste stream compositions by weight and volume from educational, administrative and dedicated purpose areas are shown in Tables 3.6, 3.7 and 3.8, respectively. Administrative areas (Table 3.7) are a source of high grade office paper as well as

Table 3.6   Educational Areas Waste Compositions

School Facility Type Basis	University of Illinois Academic (Volume %)	Northwestern University Academic (Weight %)	Dartmouth College Science (Weight %)	Dartmouth College Classrooms/Offices (Weight %)
Aluminum	1.0	3.3	1.7	2.8
Food	-	7.4	4.8	4.9
Glass	1.0	4.8	1.4	9.0
Landscape Waste	7.0 [a]	-	b	b
Metals (not inc. aluminum)	1.0	b	1.6	1.1
Paper				
Colored Paper	-	1.7	2.7	1.3
High Grade Office Paper	20.0	16.9	13.8	11.3
Mixed Paper	40.0	26.3	d	d
Other Paper	-	b	22.0	51.9
Old Corrugated Cardboard	20.0	4.4	1.5	2.6
Old Magazines	-	1.8	d	d
Old Newsprint	2.0	11.0	2.6	5.7
Paper Subtotal	82.0	62.1	42.6	72.8
Plastic				
Film (typically trash bags)	-	b	1.6	1.8
PS Foam	-	1.5	0.4	1.1
HDPE	-	c	0.1	0.0
PET	-	0.6	0.3	1.7
Other Plastic	-	7.0	3.0	3.2
Plastic Subtotal	2.0	9.1	5.4	7.8
Wood	-	-	b	b
Other	6.0	13.4	42.6 [e]	1.6
Total	100	100	100	100
Refuse Sampled (lbs.)	-	204	1298	1220
Source of Data	UIUC, 1989	NU, 1990	DC, 1988	DC, 1988

a. Includes food waste.
b. Included as part of "Other."
c. Included with PET.
d. Included as part of "Other Paper."
e. Nearly all of this value (97%) is unclassified other organics.

Table 3.7   Administrative Areas Waste Compositions

School Facility Type Basis	Northwestern University Administrative (Weight %)	Dartmouth College Administrative (Weight %)	University of Michigan Admin./Academic (Weight %)
Aluminum	4.4	1.0	a
Food	7.8	5.7	b
Glass	5.0	1.1	2.0
Landscape Waste	-	b	-
Metals (not inc. aluminum)	b	0.3	1.0
Paper			
Colored Paper	1.9	6.2	c
High Grade Office Paper	22.6	20.8	55.0
Other Paper [a]	18.0	36.7	20.0
Old Corrugated Cardboard	4.1	3.4	5.0
Old Magazines	1.1	c	c
Old Newsprint	11.5	18.3	9.0
Paper Subtotal	59.2	85.3	89.0
Plastic			
Film (typically trash bags)	-	2.2	-
PS Foam	0.2	0.5	-
HDPE	d	0.0	-
PET	0.9	0.1	-
Other Plastic	b	2.2	-
Plastic Subtotal	1.1	5.1	b
Wood	-	b	b
Other	22.5	1.5	8.0
Total	100	100	100
Refuse Sampled (lbs.)	121	1,137	-
Source of Data	NU, 1990	DC, 1988	UM

a. Included as part of metals.
b. Included as part of "Other."
c. Included as part of "Other Paper"
d. Included with PET.

Table 3.8   Specialty Areas Waste Compositions

School Facility Type Basis	University of Michigan Food Service (Volume %)	Dartmouth College Computer Center (Weight %)	Dartmouth College Libraries (Weight %)	Dartmouth College Cafeteria (Weight %)
Aluminum	a	2.4	3.0	1.4
Food	10	1.0	1.8	41.5
Glass	4	0.0	3.5	2.9
Landscape Waste	-	b	b	b
Metals (not inc. aluminum)	21	0.0	0.2	2.1
Paper				
Colored Paper	-	2.0	3.1	0.1
High Grade Office Paper	0	52.7	23.3	0.3
Mixed Paper	16	c	c	c
Other Paper	-	31.3	36.3	20.7
Old Corrugated Cardboard	33	5.8	6.9	9.5
Old Magazines	-	c	c	c
Old Newsprint	0	1.7	15.6	0.8
Paper Subtotal	49	93.5	85.2	31.4
Plastic				
Film (typically trash bags)	-	0.7	1.7	11.9
PS Foam	-	1.0	1.1	0.0
HDPE	-	0.0	0.0	0.4
PET	-	0.0	0.1	3.4
Other Plastic	-	1.0	2.9	4.6
Plastic Subtotal	7	2.7	5.7	20.3
Wood	-	b	b	b
Other	9	0.3	0.6	0.4
Total	100	100	100	100
Refuse Sampled (lbs.)	-	195	788	1480
Source of Data	UM, 1989	DC, 1988	DC, 1988	DC, 1988

a. Included with metals.
b. Included as part of "Other."
c. Included as part of "Other Paper."

newsprint, comprising an average 22% and 14% by weight respectively, for the Northwestern University and Dartmouth College waste sorts. Because dedicated purpose areas such as libraries and computer centers produce a relatively homogeneous and predictable waste stream, an emphasis should be placed on recycling at such facilities. They are a source of high grade office paper (white ledger and computer printout, Table 3.8).

Academic facilities such as science buildings generate a high quantity of paper and also more unique wastes. For example, the Dartmouth College science buildings' waste sort was comprised of 40% organic materials by weight, which do not fall into the typical categories of a waste sort.

3.3.3 Residential Areas Waste Compositions

Waste stream compositions by weight and volume from varying college living facilities are shown in Table 3.9. For the two weight based measurements (Northwestern University and Dartmouth College), junk paper (including magazines) comprises an average of 23%, ONP 17%, and food waste 10%.

3.4 Monthly Recycling Stream Variation

Recyclable quantities can vary significantly from month to month. Monitoring monthly collection amounts over a number of years can assist in a number of ways. It will: i) provide an expectation of future monthly performance, ii) identify time periods for conducting educational campaigns and special target programs, iii) identify appropriate monthly staffing levels, and iv) identify similarities among recyclable components collected or waste disposal quantities (i.e., which components exhibit the same variations).

Shown in Figures 3.4 and 3.5 are monthly three year averages of recyclable components collected at Rutgers University in New Jersey, expressed as a percentage of annual total. Over the years 1988, 1989, and 1990, the college has annually diverted 2600 tons of the 7800 tons of waste generated. The campus recycles mixed paper, corrugated cardboard, glass, aluminum containers, plastic containers and food waste. In reviewing these figures it should be noted that the two components of mixed paper and food waste comprise 32% and 44%, respectively, of all recyclables collected and therefore primary consideration should be given to their variability. Figure 3.4 shows monthly generation patterns are very similar for the components of plastics, OCC, and food waste. Peak generation of these recyclables occurs during the normal months of the school year: September - November and February - May. Down periods include June - August and January. Figure 3.5 additionally shows monthly trends for Rutgers' mixed paper and glass/cans. These components bear no similarity to the pattern in Figure 3.4. However, in

Table 3.9 Residential Areas Waste Compositions

School Facility Type Basis	Northwestern University Residence Halls (Weight %)	Dartmouth College Dormitories (Weight %)	University of Michigan Residence Halls (Volume %) Loose	University of Michigan Family Housing (Volume %) Loose	University of Illinois Housing (Volume %) Loose
Aluminum	1.6	4.7	a	a	3
Food	12.2	7.1	4.0	20.0	b
Glass	4.6	20.1	4.5	2.1	3
Landscape Waste	-	b	-	-	10[c]
Metals (not inc. aluminum)	0.0	0.2	11.2	3.0	3
Paper					
Colored Paper	1.3	3.7	-	-	-
High Grade Office Paper	4.5	3.7	2.5	10.0	10
Mixed Paper	d	d	23.7	30.0	10
Other Paper	14.1	25.1	-	-	-
Old Corrugated Cardboard	9.2	4.6	24.5	7.9	30
Old Magazines	7.2	d	-	-	-
Old Newsprint	15.9	18.0	18.1	20.0	2
Paper Subtotal	52.2	55.1	68.8	67.9	52
Plastic					
Film [e]	-	3.4	-	-	-
PS Foam	0.3	1.6	-	-	-
HDPE	f	0.0	-	-	-
PET	3.2	0.3	-	-	-
Other Plastic	b	4.0	-	-	-
Plastic Subtotal	3.5	9.4	5.4	2.0	12
Wood	-	b	b	b	-
Other (Non-Recyclables)	26.0	3.5	6.1	5.0	17
Total	100	100	100	100	100
Refuse Sampled (lbs.)	179	561	-	-	-
Source of Data	NU, 1990	DC, 1988	UM, 1989	UM, 1989	UIUC, 1988

a. Included with metals
b. Included as part of "Other"
c. Includes food waste
d. Included as part of "Other Paper"
e. Typically trash bags
f. Included with PET

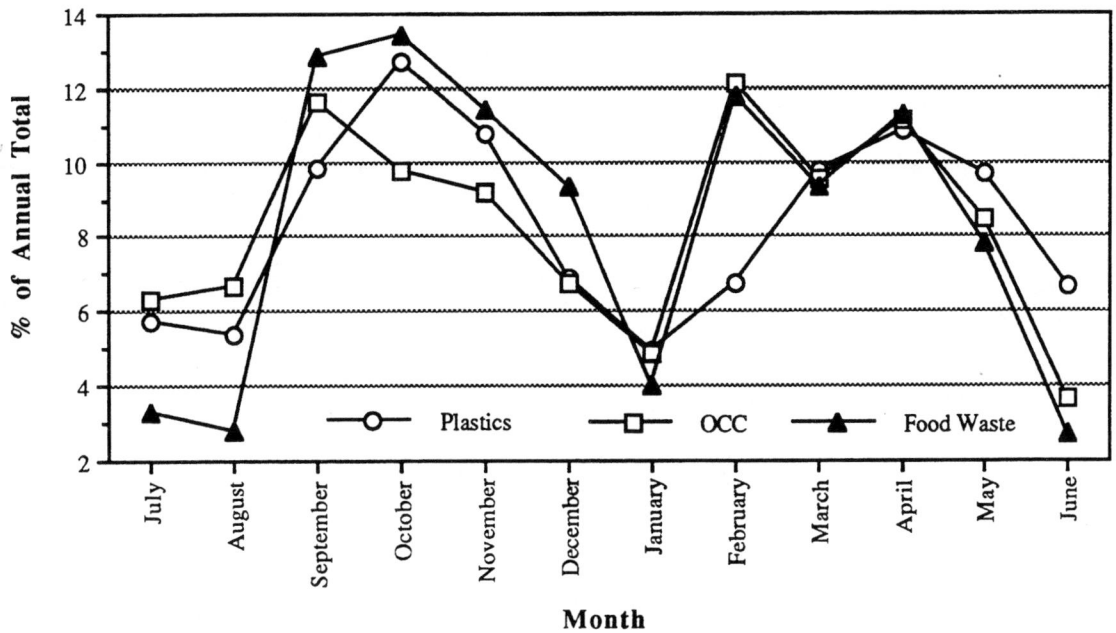

Figure 3.4 Monthly Variation in Plastics, Old Corrugated Cardboard (OCC) and Food Waste in the Rutgers University Recycling Program (Ching, 1991). Three year average shown.

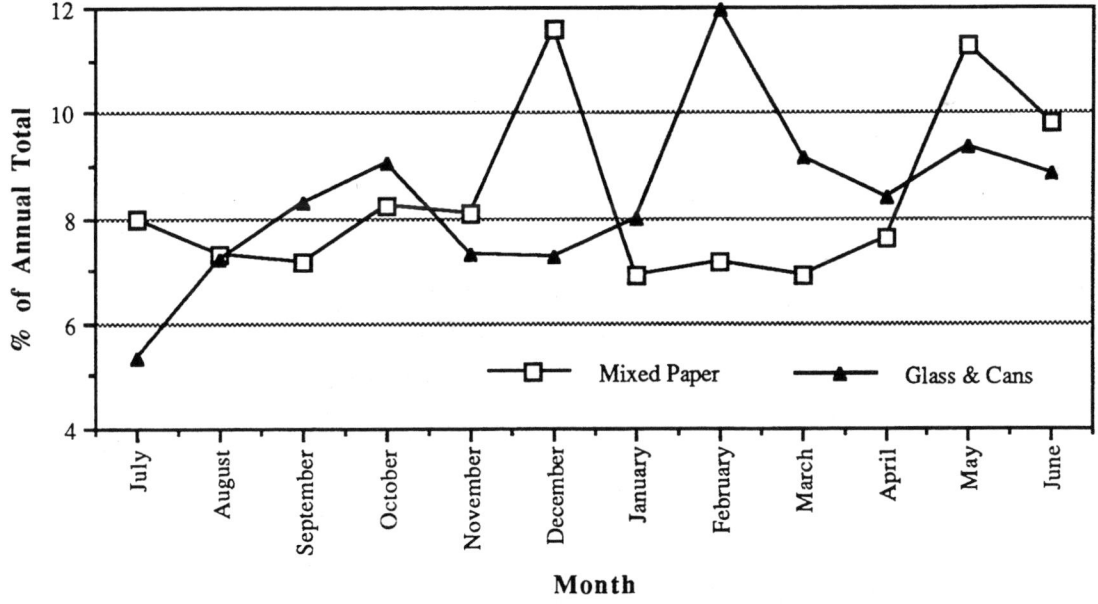

Figure 3.5 Monthly Variation in Mixed Paper, Glass and Cans in the Rutgers University Recycling Program (Ching, 1991). Three year average shown.

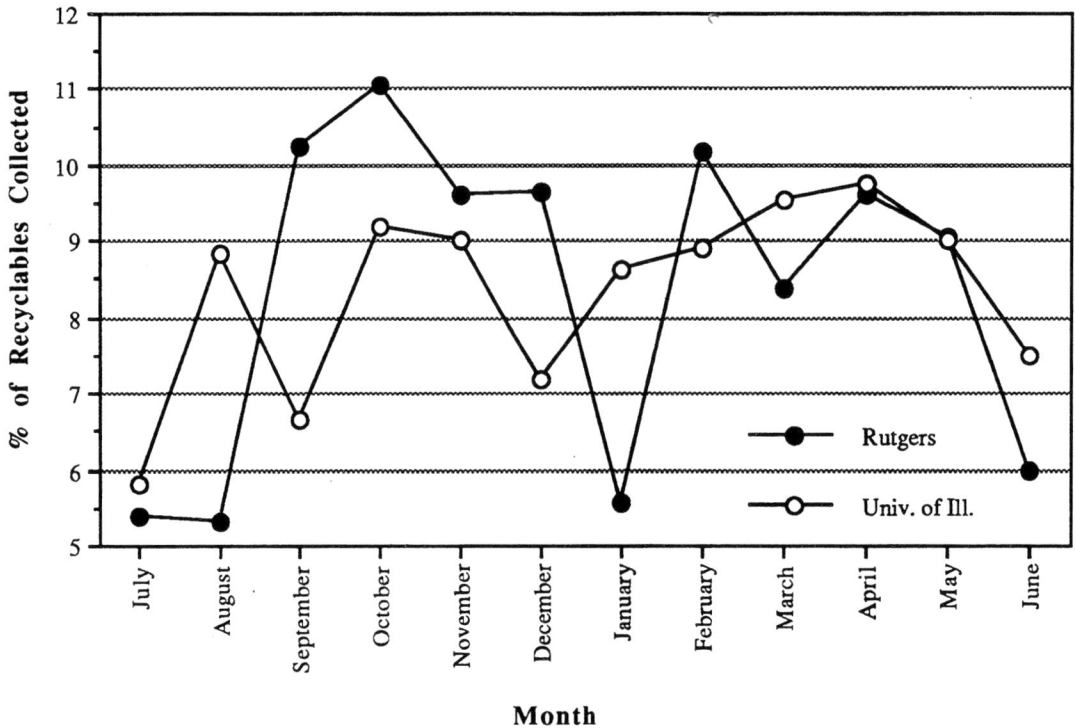

Figure 3.6 Monthly Variation of All Recyclables Collected at University of Illinois-Urbana and Rutgers University. Three year average for Rutgers and two year average for University of Illinois-Urbana shown.

conjunction with the end of each school semester, mixed paper peaks in December and May. Mixed paper remains below average generation during the remaining months.

While Figures 3.4 and 3.5 exhibit logical monthly variations, each school will be somewhat different. This is illustrated in Figure 3.6, which shows monthly quantities of all recyclables collected at the University of Illinois-Urbana and Rutgers University, expressed as a percentage of annual total. Even though both schools are on the semester type schedule, they exhibit little similarity. Monitoring of such variations on a per school basis will permit accurate estimation and the benefits detailed above.

3.5 College Recycling Generation Rates

Rates of college recycling from colleges with nearly campus-wide recycling programs are shown in Table 3.10. The rates are on a per enrolled student basis and typically show the latest year for which information was available. Because each college collects somewhat different materials and because accounting practices are somewhat different (i.e., volume based monitoring rather than weight based monitoring), not all data

Table 3.10   Recyclable Generation Rates for College Settings

Recyclable Type	Unit Recycling Rate (lb/student/year)		Source of Data
Beverage Cans			
University of Illinois-Urbana [a]	0.927		UIUC, 1991
University of Minnesota [b]	0.221		UMMS, 1990
Corrugated Cardboard			
University of Illinois-Urbana [a]	20.0		UIUC, 1991
Rutgers University	17.1		Ching, 1991
University of Minnesota [b]	19.4		UMMS, 1990
University of Michigan [c]	19.0		UMAA, 1991
Average	18.8	lb/student/year	
Food Waste			
Rutgers University	71.9		Ching, 1991
Glass			
University of Illinois-Urbana [a]	2.49		UIUC, 1991
University of Minnesota [b]	0.653		UMMS, 1990
Metals (not inc. aluminum)			
University of Minnesota [b]	0.692		UMMS, 1990
N.C. State University at Raleigh	11.5		Franks, 1991
Paper			
University of Illinois-Urbana [a]	38.3		UIUC, 1991
Rutgers University	52.2		Ching, 1991
University of Minnesota [b,d]	34.5		UMMS, 1990
University of Michigan [c,e]	42.7		UMAA, 1991
Average	41.9	lb/student/year	
Plastics			
University of Illinois-Urbana [a]	0.168		UIUC, 1991
Rutgers University	1.02		Ching, 1991
Yard Waste			
University of Minnesota [b]	9.08		UMMS, 1990
N.C. State University at Raleigh	61.5		Franks, 1991

a. FY 91 results used. Program started in 1988.
b. 1989 results used. Program started in 1984.
c. FY 91 results used. Program started in 1989.
d. Includes office paper (54.0%), newsprint (32.1%), and phonebooks (13.9%).
e. Includes mixed and white office paper (60.2%) and newsprint (39.8%).

from colleges are useful. Some waste components exhibit wide variation from college to college, such as metals and yard waste, because the activities performed or the size of a campus dictates quantities and types of waste generated.

Table 3.10 does show that for the frequently collected materials of paper (office paper, newsprint) and corrugated cardboard, about 42 lbs/student/year and 19 lbs/student/year respectively, can be expected from recycling. Once again, as with Table 3.1 these rates include the disposal on the parts of faculty and staff, as well as students. Since the colleges listed under the paper and corrugated cardboard sections of Table 3.10 have administration committed, relatively aggressive programs, these recovery rates are at the high end of what may be expected for a recycling program which is relatively new. The recycling rate of 42 lb/student/year for paper is substantially less than employee office paper recycling rates of 0.5 lb/employee/day (130 lb/employee/year, USEPA, 1990; GCRIC, 1990), particularly when estimating there is an additional 0.5 faculty/staff for each student.

The corrugated cardboard and paper rates shown in Table 3.10 provide no indication of what proportion of the amount generated is actually recovered for recycling (i.e., the recovery rate). Assuming average student waste generation for a large school of 35,000 is approximately 600 lb/student/year (Figure 3.3) and paper products (including corrugated) comprise 61% by weight (section 3.3.1), the recovery rate of all paper products generated is (42 lb. paper +19 lb. corrugated) / (0.61 • 600) • 100% = 16.7%. Therefore only 16.7% of all waste paper is actually captured in the recycling program. This indicates a large portion of paper products, even at schools with exemplary recycling programs compared to other schools, are still disposed in the municipal waste stream. This is due in large part to the portion of difficult-to-recycle "mixed" or "other" junk paper stream. It is necessary to establish an effective market and use for such material in order to maximize recycling. This also indicates it is necessary to make recycling as simplistic as possible, for maximum integration into normal daily activities. Students, staff and faculty must additionally realize that while convenience is no doubt an important factor, they may also need to make an effort and change normal activities to maximize capture rates. Lastly, recoveries of all materials vary according to such factors as level of recycling eduction, number of collection sites, and level of public interface.

4. Assessing Available Markets for Recyclables

It is extremely important to consider the markets for recyclables to be collected when planning a recycling program. The collection, processing, and education activities must be designed to meet the requirements of the markets. For example, don't collect high grade white office paper mixed with colored paper if the available markets prefer the two separated. On the other hand, some markets would prefer newsprint mixed with magazines. Programs must assess the market for recyclables in the planning stages and must also be flexible enough to meet changing market requirements.

4.1 Finding the Right Recyclable Materials Dealers

As a foremost consideration, it is necessary to establish a commitment from a recycled materials dealer who will provide consistent, quality service for the college's recyclable materials. Price paid for recyclable materials should be a secondary consideration to service when evaluating recycling companies/brokers. There are three different ways in which to obtain outlets for recyclables collected: i) a contract with a broker or dealer, who often works with a number of end-use buyers and may/may not perform intermediate processing services; ii) a contract with the end-user (such as a paper mill); or iii) open trading, whereby the producer sells to the highest bidder and there is no contract. While each has its own advantages and disadvantages, the last option (item iii) is generally not recommended because of price volatility, market gluts, and specification changes. A fourth option, the forming of a marketing cooperative followed by contract development of item i or ii above, is another intermediate variation possible. Example agreements for marketing waste paper are shown in Appendix G. Additional insight on this is available from the EPA's Marketing Waste Paper Handbook (USEPA, 1991a).

Prior to issuing a formal solicitation to bid on recycling broker/collection services, a survey of potential buyers should be conducted. The questions below will assist in conducting the survey and making an informed decision about choosing a recyclable materials dealer. While the questions specifically apply to paper, they may be utilized for collection of any recyclable. Such specifics should also be included in the final contract agreement as necessary:

1. What grades of paper are accepted and what is the minimum amount required for pickup?

2. What levels of contractor processing are available?

3. Is the dealer willing to sign a long-term contract (minimum 1 year contract recommended)?

4. What are the allowable contamination levels for non-specified paper and non-paper materials?

5. Will the dealer collect paper from each building or is it necessary to establish a central receiving area?

6. Will the dealer provide scheduled pickups, on-call pickups, or both?

7. Are destruction services available for confidential documents? Does the service meet the legal requirements required by the college?

8. Will the dealer pay for paper collected by grade classification and what is the payment frequency?

9. What pricing structure is used? For example:

    a. Floating point price tied to a paper industry market index, with a minimum floor price (most often used method because it ensures the best deal for the client and the dealer).

    b. Fixed price set for the term of the contract.

    c. Periodic review with negotiated adjustment of prices.

10. Will the dealer help organize and promote the program?

11. Is it possible to supply central recycling containers, dumpsters, and main storage bins?

12. Does the dealer require a loading dock?

13. What are the specifications for delivery of recyclable materials (e.g., baled, loose in barrels, non-shredded)?

Potential buyers of aluminum, steel, and bi-metal cans, glass containers, batteries, used oil, paper and paperboard, tires and plastics are listed in the following publications:

Title	Number	Length
Illinois Recycled Materials Market Directory	ILENR/RR-87/01	84 pp.
Directory of Illinois Recycling Centers	ILENR/RR-87/03	2 Volumes
Technologies for Recycling Post-Consumer Mixed Plastics	OTT-8	115 pp.
Used Oil Management in Illinois	OTT-10	107 pp.

ENR publications may be requested by phone at (800) 252-8955 (in Illinois) or by writing to ENR, Office of Recycling and Waste Reduction, 325 W. Adams St., Springfield, IL, 62704. University of Illinois OTT publications are available from the address shown in the front of this report.

4.2 Dealers and Mill Consumers of Waste Paper

Successful marketing of waste paper is likely to be the largest single contributor toward meeting the recycling goals for Illinois colleges and universities. Tables 4.1, 4.2, and 4.3 at the end of this chapter present a directory of paper mills consuming waste paper, producers of cellulose insulation, and paper dealers, respectively. The tables are a combined list available from the American Paper Institute and the USEPA. It should be noted that because of the volatility of the waste paper market, the list may change frequently. There are many more possible outlets listed in the tables than can be contacted in a market survey and therefore it would be prudent to survey local individuals involved in recycling for input.

4.3 Rural Area Markets

Distances to markets from rural areas of Illinois is a difficult problem. This is particularly true for community colleges which are located in such areas, have smaller operating budgets than universities, and generate recyclables at a lower rate than large schools. Because buyers for recyclables may be hundreds of miles away, cost-cutting measures should be attempted. One method could be to develop a multi-school cooperative in the same locality which would arrange for marketing of bulk recyclables. Implicit in this method is the collection of the same materials at all schools to increase overall quantity and marketability. Another method is backhauling recyclables to market in metropolitan centers such as St. Louis, Indianapolis or Chicago after receiving a shipment from such an area.

Table 4.1 Markets for Waste Paper in Illinois and Neighboring States (API,1990; EPA,1991a)

State/Company	City	Telephone	Mixed	ONP	OCC	OMG	High
Illinois							
FSC Paper Company	Alsip	(708) 389-8520	•	•		•	•
Jefferson Smurfit Corporation	Alton	(618) 463-6212	•	•	•		•
The Davey Company	Aurora	(708) 898-4231	•				
Chicago Paperboard Corp.	Chicago	(312) 997-3131	•	•	•		
Ivex Corporation	Joliet	(815) 740-3838	•		•		
Manville Sales Corporation	Joliet	(815) 744-2013		•			
Ivex Corporation	Peoria	(309) 686-3830		•			
Quaker Oats Company	Pekin	(309) 346-4118	•	•	•	•	•
Celotex Corporation	Quincy	(217) 224-3800		•	•		•
Sonoco Products Company	Rockton	(815) 624-8891	•	•	•		
Sealed Air Corporation	Salem	(618) 548-3370		•			
Indiana							
Kieffer Paper Mills, Inc.	Brownstown	(812) 358-4150	•	•	•	•	
Jefferson Smurfit Corp. (CCA)	Carthage	(317) 565-6111			•		
Rock-Tenn Company	Eaton	(317) 396-9243	•	•	•		
Georgia-Pacific Corporation	Gary	(219) 882-1640			•		•
Packaging Corp. of America	Griffith	(219) 924-4105			•		
Keyes Fibre Company	Hammond	(219) 844-8950		•	•		
Visy Recycle	Hartford City	(317) 348-0880	•	•	•		
Beveridge Paper Company	Indianapolis	(317) 635-4391		•	•		
Jefferson Smurfit Corporation	Lafayette	(317) 423-5631	•	•	•		
Inland Container Corporation	Newport	(317) 492-3341			•		
The Weston Paper & Mfg. Co	Terre Haute	(812) 234-6688			•		
Globe Building Materials	Whiting	(312) 374-5011		•	•		
Michigan							
Michigan Paperboard	Battle Creek	(616) 963-4004	•	•	•		•
Waldorf Simplex Products Group	Battle Creek	(616) 963-5511	•	•	•		•
Waldorf-Simplex Products	Constantine	(616) 435-2425	•	•	•		
Packaging Corp. of America	Filer City	(616) 723-9951			•		
Nuwool Insulation	Hudsonville	(616) 669-0100		•			
Georgia-Pacific Corporation	Kalamazoo	(616) 382-2890				•	•
James River Corporation	Kalamazoo	(616) 383-5000	•	•	•		•
Celotex Corporation	L'Anse	(906) 524-6101	•	•			•
Manistique Papers	Manistique	(906) 341-2175		•		•	
Menominee Paper Co. Inc.	Menominee	(906) 863-5595			•		
Jefferson Smurfit Corporation	Monroe	(313) 241-7776	•	•			
Monroe Paper Company	Monroe	(313) 241-7700	•	•	•		
French Paper Company	Niles	(616) 683-3025					•
Simplicity Pattern Company Inc.	Niles	(616) 683-4100	•				
Applegate Insulation	Okemos	(517) 349-9200	•	•			•
Stone Container Corporation	Ontonagon	(906) 884-2021			•		
Menasha Corporation	Otsego	(616) 692-6141			•		
Rock-Tenn Company	Otsego	(616) 692-6211	•			•	
Big M Paperboard Inc.	Palmyria	(517) 263-5160	•	•	•		
James River Corporation	Rochester	(313) 651-8121			•		
Midwest Folding Carton	Rockford	(616) 866-3421		•	•		•

Table 4.1 (cont.)

State/Company	City	Telephone	Mixed	ONP	OCC	OMG	High
Michigan (cont.)							
White Pigeon Paper Company	White Pigeon	(616) 483-7601	•	•	•		
Minnesota							
Certaineed Corporation	Shakopee	(612) 445-6450	•	•			
Waldorf Corporation	St. Paul	(612) 641-4398	•	•	•		
Ohio							
Certaineed Corporation	Avery	(419) 499-2581	•	•			
Fairfield Paper Company, L.P.	Baltimore	(614) 862-4161			•		
Ivex Corporation	Chagrin Falls	(216) 247-5530					•
Cincinnati Paperboard Corp.	Cincinnati	(513) 871-7112	•		•		
Rock-Tenn Company	Cincinnati	(513) 533-2154	•		•		
Jefferson Smurfit Corporation	Circleville	(614) 474-2146			•		
Stone Container Corporation	Coshocton	(614) 622-6543			•		
Georgia-Pacific Corporation	Franklin	(513) 746-9941	•	•			
Newark Box Board Company	Franklin	(513) 746-6493	•	•	•		•
USG Industries Inc.	Gypsum	(419) 734-3161	•	•	•		
Sonoco Products Company	Lancaster	(614) 653-6442	•	•	•		
Jefferson Smurfit Corporation	Lockland	(513) 821-2090	•	•	•		
Cleaners Hanger Company	Massillon	(216) 837-5151			•		
Greif Board Corporation	Massillon	(216) 879-2101	•	•			
Jefferson Smurfit Corporation	Middletown	(513) 422-2772	•	•	•		
Mosinee Paper Corporation	Middletown	(513) 420-5300	•	•	•		•
Newark Box Board Company	Middletown	(513) 422-6641	•	•	•		
Sonoco Products Company	Munroe Falls	(216) 688-6434	•	•	•		
Packaging Corp. of America	Rittman	(216) 925-0222	•	•	•		
Valley Converting Company	Toronto	(614) 537-2152	•	•	•		
Appleton Papers Inc.	West Carrollton	(513) 859-8261					•
Pentair Inc. (Miami Paper Corp.)	West Carrollton	(513) 859-5101					•
Wisconsin							
Riverside Paper	Appleton	(414) 749-2200					•
Beloit Box Board Company	Beloit	(608) 365-2576	•	•	•		
Globe Building Materials, Inc.	Cornell	(715) 239-6424		•	•		
U.S. Paper Mills Corporation	De Pere	(414) 336-2472	•		•		
Pope & Talbot Inc.	Eau Claire	(715) 834-3461					•
Fiberform Containers	Germantown	(414) 253-3660		•	•		
Fort Howard Corporation	Green Bay	(414) 435-8821	•	•	•	•	•
Green Bay Packaging Inc.	Green Bay	(414) 433-5000			•		
James River Corporation	Green Bay	(414) 499-0641	•				•
Pope & Talbot Inc.	Ladysmith	(715) 532-5541					•
James River Corporation	Menasha	(414) 729-8000					•
Wisconsin Tissue Corporation	Menasha	(414) 725-7031		•			
U.S. Paper Mills Corporation	Menasha	(414) 725-7115	•		•		
Ward Paper	Merrill	(715) 536-5591					•
Wisconsin Paperboard Corp.	Milwaukee	(414) 271-9000	•	•	•		
P.H. Glatfelter Company	Neenah	(414) 727-2200					•
Consolidated Paper	Stevens Point	(715) 345-8000	•	•			•

Table 4.2   Users of Newsprint for Manufacture of Cellulose Insulation

State/Organization	City	Telephone
Illinois		
Dream Home Insulation	Decatur	(217) 428-8823
American Cellulose Manufacturing	Minonk	(309) 432-2507
Insul-Mor Manufacturing	Oregon	(815) 732-7973
Indiana		
Energy Control, Inc.	Ossian	(219) 622-7614
Regal Industries	Crothersville	(812) 669-0100
Michigan		
Applegate Insulation Systems, Inc.	Okemos	(517) 349-0466
Nu-Wool Insulation Company, Inc.	Hudsonville	(616) 669-0100
Minnesota		
Energy Zone Cellulose	Buffalo	(612) 682-5755
Paul's Insulation	Vergas	(218) 342-2800
Ohio		
Electra Manufacturing/Forest Wool	Wauseon	(419) 337-4085
Central Fiber Corporation	Canton	(216) 499-3277
American Cellulose Corporation	Hamilton	(513) 863-2699
Dayton Fiber, Inc.	West Carrollton	(513) 866-5511
Ohio Cellulose Energy Corp.	Warren	(216) 392-4861
FiberChem, Inc.	Bucyrus	(419) 562-0780
International Cellulose Corp.	Monroe	(513) 539-9226
USF Corporation	Delphos	(419) 692-7015
Wisconsin		
Modern Insulation, Inc.	Spencer	(715) 659-2446
American Insulation Company	Bloomer	(715) 568-3898
Champion Insulation, Inc.	Lomira	(414) 269-4311

Table 4.3   Waste Paper Dealers in Illinois and Surrounding States

State/Company	Street	City	Zip	Telephone
<u>Illinois</u>				
Fibers, Inc.	2130 Corporate Dr.	Addison	60101	(708) 543-7676
Smurfit Recycling Co.	401 Alton St.	Alton	62002	(618) 463-6098
Paper Recovery	36 E. Dundee Road	Barrington	60010	(708) 382-6277
Belleville Recycling, Inc.	501 Hecker	Belleville	62221	(618) 233-2425
Harris Silver & Sons	800 E. Pleasant	Blevidere	61008	(815) 544-9221
Scrapman Enterprises	754 Foster Ave.	Bensenville	60106	(708) 297-0088
Midwest Paper Stock Co.	1712 S. Bunn	Bloomington	61701	(309) 829-6331
Community Recycling Center	720 N. Market St.	Champaign	61820	(217) 351-4495
Twin City Recycling Service	2808 N. Lincoln Ave.	Urbana	61801	(217) 328-2153
Kurt Sandrisser Paper Co.	101 Washington	Charleston	61920	(217) 345-2772
Airline Paper Industries	2305 S. Halsted	Chicago	60608	(312) 733-1675
Alco Salvage & Recycling	1012 S. Fairfield	Chicago	60608	(312) 638-5070
Atlas Recycling, Inc	2432 W. Barry	Chicago	60618	(312) 935-3747
Avid Sales Corp.	1820 W. 14th	Chicago	60608	(312) 226-6896
Carroll Paper Recovery	1220 W. Carroll	Chicago	60607	(312) 829-5741
Channeled Resources, Inc.	935 W. Chestnut #405	Chicago	60622	(312) 733-4200
Chicago Paperboard Corp.	900 N. Ogden	Chicago	60622	(312) 997-3131
Chicago Recycling Works, Inc.	9204 Commercial Ave. Room 211	Chicago	60617	(312) 731-8211
Columbia Paper Corp.	311 W. Superior	Chicago	60610	(312) 943-4433
Continental Paper Grading	1623 S. Lumber	Chicago	60616	(312) 226-2010
D&D Disposal	2401 Laflin	Chicago	60616	(312) 942-0029
David Holtzman	400 N. Morgan	Chicago	60622	(312) 829-8850
Donco Paper Supply Co.	737 N Michigan #1550	Chicago	60611	(312) 337-7822
Father & Son Salvage	626 E. 111th	Chicago	60628	(312) 264-3516
Flood Brother Disposal System	4827 West Harrison	Chicago	60644	(312) 626-5800
Friedland Industries, Inc.	180 N. La Salle	Chicago	60601	(312) 704-1200
Great Lakes Secondary	3702 W. 38th	Chicago	60632	(312) 927-0209
Herman Bailen	6349 N. Western	Chicago	60659	(312) 973-2433
Howard Zuker Associates	875 N. Michigan	Chicago	60611	(312) 664-5700
Huron Paper Stock Co.	2545 W. Fulton	Chicago	60612	(312) 829-7456
Illinois Scrap	2048 W. Hubbard	Chicago	60612	(312) 421-0563
Intercel	3110 W. 28th Street	Chicago	60623	(312) 847-8000
James Flett Organization, Inc.	20 N. Wacker Dr.	Chicago	60606	(312) 726-0950
JB Scrap Metal	2910 Carroll	Chicago	60612	(312) 533-4200
Lakewood Recycling Center	1305 W. Belmont	Chicago	60657	(312) 472-4800
Leader Box Corp.	963 W. Cullerton	Chicago	60608	(312) 226-2622
Loop Recycling, Inc.	2401 S. Laflin	Chicago	60608	(312) 942-0042
Lynn & Co.,Div. Northwest Slvg.	4519 W. Patterson St.	Chicago	60641	(312) 545-7560
Marcells Paper & Metal, Inc.	2318 W. Devon Ave.	Chicago	60659	(312) 465-8864
Mid-America Paper Co., Inc.	1144 S. Fairfield	Chicago	60612	(312) 826-5046
National Fiber Supply Co.	55 E. Monroe	Chicago	60603	(312) 346-4800
National Paper Grading Co.	6901 S. Bell Ave.	Chicago	60636	(312) 436-4546
Northwest Salvage Co.	4519 W. Patterson	Chicago	60641	(312) 545-7560

Table 4.3   Waste Paper Dealers in Illinois and Surrounding States (cont.)

State/Company	Street	City	Zip	Telephone
<u>Illinois (cont.)</u>				
Paper Chase Exchange Inc.	3730 S. St. Louis	Chicago	60632	(312) 247-2700
Paper Group	2901 W. 36th Place	Chicago	60632	(312) 376-8341
Paper Salvage Corp.	655 W. Irving Park Rd., Suite 111	Chicago	60613	(312) 248-2070
Profile Document Processing	6600 W. Armitage	Chicago	60635	(312) 237-7200
Recycling Services, Inc.	4800 S. Morgan	Chicago	60609	(312) 247-2070
S. Gordon & Sons	1727 S. Stewart Ave	Chicago	60616	(312) 421-6111
Skokie Valley Shipping	2142 W. Carroll	Chicago	60612	(312) 666-2888
Unique Salvage	1039 N. La Salle	Chicago	60610	(312) 951-5300
Waste Reclaiming Co.	2121 W. Carroll	Chicago	60612	(312) 243-3470
West Pullman Iron/Metal	11954 S. Peoria	Chicago	60643	(312) 785-0534
Western Fibers Inc.	201 N. Wells	Chicago	60606	(312) 630-0120
Wolf Mill Supply Co.	6901 S. Bell	Chicago	60636	(312) 436-4546
Cicero Iron Metal/Paper	5901 Ogden	Cicero	60650	(312) 863-8601
Decatur Recycle Paper	2500 N. M L King Jr. Dr.	Decatur	62526	(217) 875-2425
Waste Control Services, Inc.	P.O. Box 1464	Decatur	62525	(312) 429-9378
Paper & Pulp Co.	2340 S. River Rd.	Des Plaines	60018	(708) 299-2027
R G Salvage & Recycling	134 E Touhy Ct.	Des Plaines	60018	(708) 803-6885
Simkin Iron & Metal, Inc.	9296 Home Terrace	Des Plaines	60018	(708) 297-6070
Father & Son Salvage	1445 Kasten	Dolton	60419	(708) 841-6440
Davis Recycling	236 N. 5th St.	East St. Louis	62201	(618) 271-6610
Solid Waste Recovery	500 N. Front	East St. Louis	62201	(618) 274-8157
Office Paper Recycling Inc.	PO Box 252	Elmhurst	60126	(708) 941-0020
Data Products Recycling	3800 Acorn	Franklin Park	60131	(708) 455-5797
Freeport Recycling Center	657 N. Van Buren	Freeport	61032	(815) 232-2906
Best Recycling Services	1912 Lehigh	Glenview	60025	(708) 724-2378
Paul Hindman's Disposal	900 N. Park Ave.	Herrin	62948	(618) 942-2025
Hillsboro Paper Stock Co.	Railroad	Hillsboro	62049	(217) 532-5941
The V.I.M. Corporation	119 E. Ogden Ave.	Hinsdale	60521	(708) 858-5180
Berlinsky Scrap Corp.	212 Page Ave.	Joliet	60432	(815) 726-4334
Mobile Document Destruction	R.R. 2	Kankakee	60901	(815) 932-3889
Rondout Iron & Metal Co.	1501 Rockland Rd.	Lake Bluff	60044	(708) 362-2750
Recycling Unlimited	108 S. Wall St.	Macon	62544	(217) 764-3371
Du Page Paper Stock Co.	1301 Greenwood Ave	Maywood	60153	(708) 343-1024
Metropolitan Fiber	1216 N. Appaloosa Tr.	McHenry	60050	(815) 344-7800
R & L Recycling Corp.	4719 Lake	Melrose Park	60160	(708) 681-3626
United Fibers Inc.	4719 West Lake St.	Melrose Park	60160	(800) 727-3750
Arlington Salvage	606 Elderberry	Mt. Prospect	60056	(708) 255-4546
Kendrick Paper Stock Co.	603 S. 12th St.	Mt. Vernon	62864	(618) 242-4527
Alan Josephsen Co., Inc.	901 E. Orchard	Mundelein	60060	(708) 949-0700
Paper/Chemical Exchange	1464 Terrence Dr.	Naperville	60565	(708) 983-5333
Hughs Recycling	RR#2	New Berlin	62670	(217) 488-6013
Edward Sider & Co.	707 Skokie Blvd.	Northbrook	60062	(708) 272-2910
Maritime Brokers	3701 Commercial Ave.	Northbrook	60062	(708) 564-4660
C&M Recycling	1600 Morrow Ave.	North Chicago	60064	(708) 578-1066
American Paper Recycling	301 W. Lake St.	Northlake	60164	(708) 344-6789

Table 4.3   Waste Paper Dealers in Illinois and Surrounding States (cont.)

State/Company	Street	City	Zip	Telephone
<u>Illinois (cont.)</u>				
Insul-Mor Mfg.	White Pines Rd.	Oregon	61061	(815) 732-7973
I Erlichman Company, Inc.	3213 SW. Washington	Peoria	61602	(309) 637-4491
Quincy Recycle Paper, Inc.	526 S. 6th	Quincy	62301	(217) 224-2754
RSVIP Ltd.	2725 N. Thatcher	River Grove	60171	(708) 452-1158
C.H. Oscarson Co. Inc.	2701 Daiquiri Drive	Riverwoods	60015	(708) 945-2246
Robins Recycling	1311 Harrison Ave.	Rockford	61104	(815) 398-2267
Rockford Maint./Recycling	2131 Harlem Road	Rockford	61111	(815) 654-0206
Durbin Paper Stock Co	430 1st. St.	Rock Island	61201	(309) 786-6633
Rondout Iron & Metal Co., Inc.	1501 Rockland Road	Rondout	60044	(708) 362-2750
Western Pacific Pulp & Paper	999 Plaza Dr. Suite 400	Schaumburg	60173	(708) 310-4482
Intensive Processing Services	515 Stevenson Dr.	South Elgin	60177	(708) 695-3328
Central Iron & Metal Co.	1100 S. Ninth St.	Springfield	62705	(217) 523-3619
H.I.S. Recycling	2130 Clearlake Ave.	Springfield	62703	(217) 788-9455
Mervis Iron & Supply	1023 E. Madison	Springfield	62703	(217) 753-1493
Waste Paper, Inc.	1501 Groth St.	Springfield	62707	(217) 544-7731
Midstate Recycling	1402 W. South St.	Taylorville	62568	(217) 824-6047
Recycled Paper Products	2510 Bond	University Park	60466	(708) 534-0041
Wheel-In-Recycling	1211 N. Garland Rd.	Wauconda	60084	(708) 526-2978
Desktop Recycling	1000 Capitol Drive	Wheeling	60090	(708) 537-3008
McHenry County Defenders	239 Throop St.	Woodstock	60098	(815) 338-0393
Shamrock Fibers, Inc.	665 Jackson St.	Woodstock	60098	(815) 338-8513
<u>Indiana</u>				
Kentuckiana Waste Paper	1507 Progress Way	Clarksville	47130	(812) 282-8856
Commercial Waste	5607 W. 101st	Crown Point	46307	(219) 769-7444
Central Baling Co.	605 Mason	Elkhart	46516	(219) 293-3751
Jefferson Smurfit Corp	1520 N. 5th Ave.	Evansville	47710	(812) 425-6279
Pioneer Fibers, Inc.	6801 Lake Plaza Dr., 105A	Fishers	46038	(317) 842-8970
All Seal Insulation, Inc.	929 Leesburg Road	Fort Wayne	46808	(219) 432-7591
Paper Recyclers, Inc.	702 Hayden	Fort Wayne	46803	(219) 426-6353
Pontiac Street Paper Station	3200 E. Pontiac	Fort Wayne	46803	(219) 424-3565
Cornelius Paper Recycling	3605 E. Terrace Ave.	Indianapolis	46203	(317) 352-8323
Covenant paper Stock, Inc.	502 S. Harris Ave.	Indianapolis	46222	(317) 638-3890
Davis Paper Co.	850 Blake Suite D	Indianapolis	46202	(317) 636-5345
Indianapolis Recycled Fiber	1775 S. West	Indianapolis	46225	(317) 634-7571
Indy Recycling	3615 Kentucky Ave.	Indianapolis	46241	(317) 244-3300
Langsdale Recycling, Inc.	832 Langsdale Ave.	Indianapolis	46202	(317) 925-5492
Pioneer Fibers Inc.	6801 Lake Plaza Dr.	Indianapolis	46229	(317) 842-8970
Royal Paper Co.	2210 Montcalm	Indianapolis	46208	(317) 631-6609
Kentucky Document Shredding	305 Missouri Ave.	Jeffersonville	47130	(812) 282-2822
Migler, Inc.	601 Uhl Dr.	Kendallville	46755	(219) 347-4739
Knox Recycling & Scrap Processing	300 W. Lake St.	Knox	46534	(219) 772-2705
River City Recycling, Inc.	2408 S. 30th	Lafayette	47905	(317) 477-6732
Riverside Recycling, Inc.	1001 Floyd	New Albany	47150	(812) 948-1323
Central States Fiber	837 Webster St.	Shelbyville	46176	(317) 282-2556
Hoosier Paper Stock, Inc.	US 421 E.	Shelbyville	46176	(317) 398-0286

Table 4.3   Waste Paper Dealers in Illinois and Surrounding States (cont.)

State/Company	Street	City	Zip	Telephone
<u>Indiana (cont.)</u>				
North Side Iron/Paper co.	3123 Gertrude St.	South Bend	46614	(219) 288-1498
South Bend Waste Paper	1519 S. Franklin	South Bend	46613	(219) 234-7181
Superior Waste Systems	20645 W. Ireland Rd.	South Bend	46614	(219) 299-0500
T.H.R.O.W., Inc.	99 Mulberry	Terre Haute	47807	(812) 232-2940
American Recycling	Highway 50 West	Washington	47501	(812) 254-1983
<u>Michigan</u>				
T. Nalepka Waste Paper Co.	5662 Platt Road	Ann Arbor	48104	(313) 429-4612
Cereal City Recycling	15160 6 1/2 Mi. Road	Battle Creek	49017	(616) 963-9814
Brady Paper Recycling	808 26th St.	Bay City	48708	(517) 892-5009
Abe Surath & Sons Inc.	1640 Marquette St.	Bay City	48707	(517) 667-0502
Thermocon Midwest	5020 W. River Dr. NE	Comstock Park	49321	(616) 784-6447
Tri-County Recycling	4000 W River Dr. NE	Comstock Park	49321	(616) 784-4466
Aaro Waste Paper Co.	14269 Goddard	Detroit	48212	(313) 893-6194
Bluestein Brothers	3195 Bellevue	Detroit	48207	(313) 922-2720
Capitol Waste Paper Co.	10571 Grand River	Detroit	48204	(313) 934-3900
Downtown Paper & Metal	2812 W. Fort	Detroit	48216	(313) 963-7664
General Mill Supply Co.	189 Vineyard	Detroit	48216	(313) 554-1000
Gillett Waste Material	1551 Gillett St.	Detroit	48211	(313) 872-7195
Intermet, Ltd.[E]	6000 Buchanan St.	Detroit	48210	(313) 894-0545
International Paper Recycling	6401 Strong	Detroit	48211	(313) 571-8400
Junction-McGregor Center	5650 McGregor	Detroit	48209	(313) 554-3705
Lafayette Recycling Corp.	7700 Dix	Detroit	48209	(313) 843-1312
Midstates Fibres, Inc.	1650 Waterman	Detroit	48209	(313) 843-8650
Midstates Fibres, Inc.	14269 Goddard	Detroit	48212	(313) 368-6703
Averill Waste, Inc.	220 S Averill	Flint	48506	(313) 767-3450
Industrial Iron/Metal Co.	4710 N. Dort	Flint	48505	(313) 785-0883
Fremont Rag & Metal	127 W. Elm	Fremont	49412	(616) 924-4930
VIP Services	55730 16th Ave.	Grand Junction	49056	(616) 427-5588
Grand Rapids Iron/Metal	57 Logan SW	Grand Rapids	49503	(616) 459-2211
Krell Paper Stock Co., Inc.	580 Burton SW	Grand Rapids	49510	(616) 245-9168
Lubbers Resource Systems	0-862 Luce	Grand Rapids	49504	(616) 453-7985
Recycle America of Michigan	1737 Chicago Dr. SW	Grand Rapids	49509	(616) 243-7191
Louis Padnos Iron & Metal Co.	120 River Ave.	Holland	49422	(616) 396-6521
Jackson Fiber & Metallic	1417 S. Elm	Jackson	49203	(517) 784-9191
James River Corporation	243 E. Paterson	Kalamazoo	49007	(616) 383-5000
R & S Supply Inc.	5526 Lover's Lane	Kalamazoo	49002	(616) 343-8771
Second Phase Recycling	1528 King Highway	Kalamazoo	49001	(616) 342-4376
Thall Associates	429 Porter	Kalamazoo	49007	(616) 385-4774
Commercial Haulers	1598 17 Mile	Kent City	49330	(616) 887-7224
Friedland Industries Inc.	314 E. Maple	Lansing	48901	(517) 482-3000
B & F Specialties	8710 Custer Road	Maybee	48159	(313) 587-8675
Jefferson Smurfit Corp.	1151 W. Elm St.	Monroe	48161	(313) 241-7776
Southeastern Fibers Inc.	214 E. Elm #106	Monroe	48161	(313) 242-9874
Brann Industries Inc.	1415 Lake	Niles	49120	(616) 683-5577
Niles Waste Paper Co.	853 N. Font	Niles	49120	(616) 683-2610

Table 4.3 Waste Paper Dealers in Illinois and Surrounding States (cont.)

State/Company	Street	City	Zip	Telephone
Michigan (cont.)				
Blue Water Cardboard	3541 32nd	Port Huron	48060	(313) 984-5545
Blue Water Recycling	2829 Gouldend	Port Huron	48060	(313) 985-6200
Nelson Paper Recycling	30880 Smith Road	Romulus	48174	(313) 721-0197
Great Lakes Paper Stock	30615 Groesbeck Hwy	Roseville	48066	(313) 779-1310
Royal Oak Waste Paper & Metal	414 E. Hudson	Royal Oak	48067	(313) 541-4020
Jackson Record Shredding	1514 S. 25th	Saginaw	48601	(517) 754-0930
Michigan Paper Stock Co.	29350 Southfield Rd.	Southfield	48076	(313) 559-4411
Taylor Recycling Inc.	8767 Holland Road	Taylor	48180	(313) 291-7410
Allan Blum Co.	4333 Westover Ct. W.	Bloomfield Twp	48033	(313) 851-9515
Fenske Enterprises	2637 Wilson SW	Walker	49504	(616) 453-3131
L & L Recycling Co. Inc.	34939 Brush	Wayne	48184	(313) 721-7436
Tipton Waste Paper Co.	1731 Cadillac	Ypsilanti	48198	(313) 485-2370
Action Dispose & Recycling	1724 Woodale	Ypsilanti Twp	48198	(313) 485-4666
Minnesota				
Howard Waste Paper Inc.	414 S. 59th Ave. West	Duluth	55807	(218) 628-2388
Recovery Systems Co., Inc.	15 10th Ave. South	Hopkins	55232	(612) 935-4330
Kato Sanitation	RFD 1	Mankato	56001	(507) 388-1157
Contamination Control	5469 Hwy 12	Maple Plain	55359	(612) 479-2829
American Iron & Supply Inc.	2800 Pacific St., North	Minneapolis	55411	(612) 529-9221
Data-Fiber Products Corporation	2400 N. 2nd St.	Minneapolis	55411	(612) 588-8554
Pioneer Paper Stock Co.	155 Irving Ave. N.	Minneapolis	55405	(612) 374-2280
Recycling Services	2600 N. 2nd St.	Minneapolis	55411	(612) 522-6558
Southeastern Fibers Inc.	511 11th Ave. S.	Minneapolis	55415	(612) 338-1748
Pythons Recycle Center	38 North 19th Ave.	St. Cloud	56301	(612) 645-5721
Bro-Tex Co.	800 Hampden Ave.	St. Paul	55114	(612) 645-5721
Great Western Iron/Metal	521 Barge Channel Road	St. Paul	55107	(612) 224-4877
Metro Paper Recovery	2785 N. Fairview Ave.	St. Paul	55113	(612) 631-1693
Rohn Industries	862 Hersey St.	St. Paul	55114	(612) 647-1300
Steve's Cardboard Salvage	381 York Ave.	St. Paul	55101	(612) 771-2383
Waldorf Corporation	2250 Wabash Ave.	St. Paul	55114	(612) 641-4938
Ohio				
Acroa Corporation	114 Anaconda Ave.	Akron	44310	(216) 633-2409
BFI Recycling	964 Hazel St.	Akron	44305	(216) 434-9183
Alliance Recycling Center	15969 River NE	Alliance	44601	(216) 821-8057
Maxwell Recycling	480 Fifth St. NE	Barberton	44203	(216) 848-1815
Bellefontaine Recycling	117 Buckingham Ave. W	Bellefontaine	43311	(513) 592-2514
Sims Bros. Inc.	668 Woodlawn AVe.	Bucyrus	44820	(419) 562-3225
Leopold Co.	2721 Harrisburg NE	Canton	44705	(216) 455-0205
Marks Paper Stock Co.	802 Navarre Road SW	Canton	44707	(216) 453-9149
S Slesnick Co.	404 Fifth St. SE	Canton	44702	(216) 454-5101
RLS Recycling	990 Eastern Ave.	Chillicothe	45601	(614) 773-1440
Accu-Pak	4620 Spring Grove Ave.	Cincinnati	45232	(513) 541-3373
Astro Recycling Co	861 Dellway St.	Cincinnati	45229	(513) 961-3500
Cinti Material Inc.	11759 Enterprise Ave.	Cincinnati	45241	(513) 772-6262

Table 4.3   Waste Paper Dealers in Illinois and Surrounding States (cont.)

State/Company	Street	City	Zip	Telephone
<u>Ohio (cont.)</u>				
Container Corp. America	1258 Knowlton St.	Cincinnato	45223	(513) 681-8200
Smurfit Recycling	1258 Knowlton St.	Cincinnati	45223	(513) 681-8200
Donco Paper Supply Co.	2100 Losantiville Ave	Cincinnati	45237	(513) 731-0208
Ecolo Fibers Paper/Metal	1441 Spring Lawn	Cincinnati	45223	(513) 542-4444
Metro Recycling Co.	2424 Beekman Ave.	Cincinnati	45214	(513) 251-1800
Acme Waste Products	4801 Chaincraft	Cleveland	44125	(216) 587-3333
All Scrap Salvage Co. Inc.	3550 W. 140th	Cleveland	44111	(216) 941-7100
Blue Sun Energy & Insulation	1109 E. 152nd St.	CLeveland	44110	(216) 761-1775
Cleveland Recyclery	2824 E. 75th St.	Cleveland	44104	(216) 391-1524
Ohio Waste Material Co.	965 Wayside Road	Cleveland	44110	(216) 481-3200
Packaging Corp-America	3400 Vega Ave.	Cleveland	44113	(216) 961-5060
Quincy Wastepaper Co.	2175 Ashland Road	Cleveland	44103	(216) 391-6866
Smith & Sons	6318 Kinsman	Cleveland	44104	(216) 391-6844
Sobel Salvage Co.	18612 Miles	Cleveland	44128	(216) 475-2100
Weiskepf Textile Co.	2824 E. 75th St.	Cleveland	44104	(216) 432-0045
Burke Waste Paper Processing	2757 W. 4th Ave.	Columbus	43201	(614) 252-7766
Burke Waste Paper Processing	1662 Williams Road	Columbus	43207	(614) 491-9380
Great Eastern Packing	805 Reynolds	Columbus	43201	(614) 299-2164
Great Eastern Packing & Stock	2771 E. 4th St.	Columbus	43219	(614) 258-1077
Grossman Industries Inc.	1960 S. 4th St.	Columbus	43207	(614) 445-8181
Ohio Waste Paper	1960 S. Fourth St.	Columbus	43207	(614) 445-8181
Prosort Inc.	1088 N. High St.	Columbus	43201	(614) 291-7119
Paper & Pulp Exchange, Inc.	3991 Fondorf Dr.	Columbus	43228	(614) 274-4857
Recycling Exchange	1015 Marion Road	Columbus	43207	(614) 445-8188
Recycling Exchange North	2830 Westerville	Columbus	43224	(614) 471-5956
Royal Paper Stock Co. Inc.	531 W. Goodale St.	Columbus	43215	(614) 224-8127
Royal Paper Stock Co. Inc.	3980 Groves Road	Columbus	43232	(614) 861-7326
United Paper Stock	2771 E. 4th Ave.	Columbus	43219	(614) 258-1077
Waste Recovery Corporation	2019 Beverly Road	Columbus	43221	(614) 486-2946
Chief Petty Paper Co.	47849 Papermill Road	Coshocton	43812	(614) 623-0368
Capitol Materials Co.	401 Washington St.	Dayton	45402	(513) 222-7479
Levy Ira & Associates	47 Macro Lane	Dayton	45458	(513) 434-7244
Montgomery Paper Co	400 E. Fourth St.	Dayton	45402	(513) 222-4059
Recycled Fibers of Ohio	2601 E. River Road	Dayton	45439	(513) 298-9969
Thoma Recycled Fibers	3840 Dayton-Xenia Road	Dayton	45432	(513) 429-9188
Elyria Paper & Salvage	460 Oberlin Road	Elyria	44035	(216) 323-9633
National Waste Paper Co.	3651 Broadway	Elyria	44039	(216) 324-6616
Normac Fibers Inc.	9265 Seward Raod	Fairfield	45014	(513) 874-0660
Sam Mindlin & Son	666 S. Riley Boulevard	Franklin	45005	(513) 746-5471
Shepaco Paper Co.	134 Vine St. PO Box 117	Hamilton	45012	(513) 863-3474
Allen County Recyclers	541 S. Central	Lima	45804	(419) 223-5010
Edith Rachlin	520 E. Pennsylvania	Lima	45801	(419) 229-7541
Milliron Auto Parts	RD #3, SR, 39 NW	Mansfield	44903	(419) 747-4566
National Waste Paper Co.	3651 Broadway	Lorain	44052	(215) 244-1806
Sims Brothers Inc.	1011 S. Prospect	Marion	43302	(614) 387-9041
Lytton Sanitation Service	603 First St.	Martins Ferry	43935	(614) 635-1861

Table 4.3   Waste Paper Dealers in Illinois and Surrounding States (cont.)

State/Company	Street	City	Zip	Telephone
<u>Ohio (cont.)</u>				
Medina Paper Recycling	370 Lake Road PO Box 561	Medina	44256	(216) 723-4334
Dayton Fiber Inc.	4200 Soldiers Home-W. Carlton Rd.	Miamisburg	45342	(513) 866-5511
Tri-State Waste Paper	521 St. Clair St.	Mingo Junction	43938	(614) 535-0301
Royal Paper Stock Co., Inc.	2601 E. River Rd.	Maraine	45439	(513) 298-9969
Mid-Ohio Recycling Center	1225 W. Gambler	Mount Vernon	43050	(614) 397-9668
Sonoco Products Co.	PO Box 211	Munroe Falls	44262	(216) 688-6434
NRG Inc.	12-471 TWP Road R	Napoleon	43545	(419) 599-1659
Slabaugh Manufacturing	3920 State NW	North Canton	44720	(216) 499-3277
Associated Paper Stock	11510 South Ave.	North Lima	44452	(216) 549-5311
Associated Paper Stock	11460 Mentzer Dr.	North Lima	44452	(216) 549-0015
Norwalk Waste Materials Co.	US Route 250 N.	Norwalk	44857	(419) 668-3341
Sussman Inc./Queen City Ind.	637 W. Water St.	Piqua	45356	(513) 773-2565
Packaging Corp, of America	Industrial Street	Rittman	44270	(216) 927-5010
Tower Metal Alloy Co.	1370 Columbus Ave.	Springfield	45503	(513) 324-0272
Recycling Station	3105 Hill Ave.	Toledo	43607	(419) 531-8828
The State Paper & Metal Co.	1118 W. Central	Toledo	43606	(419) 243-5567
Toledo Paper Stock Co.	1510 Elm St.	Toledo	43608	(419) 243-3215
Charles W. Hall	111 N. Vine	Van Wert	45891	(419) 238-5476
Cartwright Salvage Co.	839 Bogus NE	Washington Ct. HS	43160	(614) 335-6344
Cartwright Salvage Co.	760 Robinson SE	Washington Ct. HS	43160	(614) 335-5361
Willoughby Iron & Waste	3884 Church	Willoughby	44094	(216) 946-8990
Metallics Recycling Inc.	1375 Old Mansfield Road	Wooster	44691	(216) 264-5455
<u>Wisconsin</u>				
Golper Supply Co.	1810 W. Edgewood Dr.	Appleton	54915	(414) 731-3266
Perry H. Koplik & Sons	200 E. Washington St.	Appleton	54911	(414) 731-3266
Riverside Materials	800 S. Lawe St.	Appleton	54912	(414) 733-3614
Unlimited Resources Inc.	4360 W. Parkway Blvd.	Appleton	54915	(414) 739-2488
Aronson Steel Products	111 Myrtle Rd.	Beaver Dam	53916	(414) 887-3232
Pelman Iron & Metal Co.	5510 S. Whitnall Ave.	Cudahy	53110	(414) 483-8833
Hansen's Recycling	421 Bloom Rd.	Eagle River	54521	(715) 479-8787
Western Dairyland Recycling	335 Putman St.	Eau Claire	54703	(715) 834-7780
Betten Processing Co.	2175 Shawnano Ave.	Green Bay	54307	(414) 494-3451
Donco Paper Supply Co.	2050 Riverside Dr.	Green Bay	54301	(414) 432-7900
EcoSource	PO Box 12481	Green Bay	54307	(414) 435-2644
Paper Processing Inc.	1315 Gate	Green Bay	54303	(414) 432-8005
Willmann Fiber	910 N. Broadway	Green Bay	54303	(414) 432-9353
Janesville Recycling Center	340 Black Bridge Rd.	Janesville	53545	(608) 756-3603
La Crosse Waste Paper Co.	500 Milwaukee	La Crosse	54603	(608) 782-1801
Ben Heifetz Inc.	1802 South Park	Madison	53707	(608) 255-0960
Madison Recycling Center	2200 Fish Hatchery Rd.	Madison	53713	(608) 251-2115
Zinkel Enterprises	1820 S. 30th	Manitowoc	54220	(414) 682-9244
American Quality Fibers Ltd.	206 Railroad	Menasha	54952	(414) 722-8010
National Fiber Supply Co.	P.O. Box 336	Menasha	54952	(414) 722-4206

Table 4.3   Waste Paper Dealers in Illinois and Surrounding States (cont.)

State/Company	Street	City	Zip	Telephone
Wisconsin (cont.)				
A-1 Recycling	2101 W. Morgan Ave.	Milwaukee	53221	(414) 281-8900
Bass Brothers Paper Inc.	3299 N. 30th	Milwaukee	53216	(414) 873-5330
Cream City Recycling Center	1516 E. Thomas Ave.	Milwaukee	53211	(414) 272-5676
Holzman & Sons	301 W. Dean Road	Milwaukee	53211	(414) 351-2124
Felex Bandos Waste Material	1132 S. Barclay	Milwaukee	53204	(414) 272-0900
Milwaukee Waste Paper Co.	2342 N. Newhall	Milwaukee	53211	(414) 271-5320
National Salvage Ltd.	6709 W. National Ave.	Milwaukee	53214	(414) 453-6677
Paper Processing Inc.	1516 E. Thomas Ave.	Milwaukee	53211	(414) 271-9030
Peltz Brothers Corporation	4875 N. 32nd	Milwaukee	53209	(414) 445-6279
Peterman Paper Process	1813 S. 66th	Milwaukee	53214	(414) 541-3100
Recycling World Inc.	3607 N. Richards	Milwaukee	53212	(414) 332-1700
Recycling World Inc.	504 W. Cherry	Milwaukee	53212	(414) 263-2626
West Allis Salvage Co.	1909 S. 80th	Milwaukee	53219	(414) 321-4134
Chuck's Recycling	N7356 Lake Shore Dr.	N. Fond Du Lac	54935	(414) 922-6400
Kard Recycling Service Inc.	2925 S. 163rd	New Berlin	53151	(414) 786-7307
Oshkosh Paper Salvage Co.	1860 Harrison	Oshkosh	54901	(414) 235-2000
Racine Salvage Corporation	1314 Frederick	Racine	53404	(414) 632-6662
Standard Scrap Metal Ltd.	1415 Durand Ave.	Racine	53403	(414) 637-2900
Marketing Associates Ltd.	430 W. Union	Richland Center	53581	(608) 647-8675
Sheboygan Waste Material	1205 Illinois Ave.	Sheboygan	53081	(414) 457-5091
Pontzloff's Salvage Co.	W607 Concord Center Dr.	Sullivan	53178	(414) 567-3301
J & M Fibers Inc.[E]	45 Ruby Lane	Sun Prarie	53590	(608) 837-5409
Mobile Shredding Services	W246 S3234 Industrial	Waukesha	53186	(414) 521-9100
Spring City Salvage Co.	931 Niagara	Waukesha	53186	(414) 547-8891
Aronson Steel Products Inc.	1350 W. Brown St.	Waupun	52963	(414) 324-2977
National Salvage Ltd.	6709 W. National Ave.	West Allis	53214	(414) 453-6677
Lynn's Waste Paper Co.	121 Island Ave.	West Bend	53095	(414) 334-9542
General Paper Stock Co.	941 Alton	Wisconsin Rapids	54494	(715) 423-0219

5. Strategies for Implementing College Waste Reduction

Reducing waste generated and recycling are the two primary strategies available for minimizing the amount of municipal waste subject to ultimate disposal. This chapter addresses approaches to reduction and recycling in general and for specific college functions.

The type of waste handled within the university dictate the different educational, collection and processing methods used. While academic area waste may expected to be mainly paper, food service waste can be expected to be food waste and container materials. Similarly, dormitory or fraternity/sorority waste would more closely parallel standard "municipal waste," albeit with increased quantities of disposable packaging. The waste from each of these examples would be handled in different fashion, and as such the differing considerations shown in this chapter should be made.

5.1 Source Reduction

Modification of work activities and procurement modifications are two primary methods of source reduction. The number of source reduction efforts which can be implemented are as numerous as there are work activities. The benefits of each reduction method must be evaluated against change in cost or services provided. Methods for source reduction which have succeeded at college campuses are shown in Table 5.1.

Procurement modification entails purchasing effectively such that total waste generated per product purchased is minimized, recyclability is maximized and/or life cycle is optimized. The following recommendations will assist in properly selecting/procuring products (UBC, 1991):

- Conduct a review of environmental impacts of products purchased.
- Adopt and promote three criteria for purchasing decision making: performance, product durability, and life cycle cost of the product.
- If life cycle cost is not feasible, procurement preference will be given to products that contribute to durability, even if cost is greater.
- Collaborate with sources of environmental purchasing information.
- Add a standard tender clause to all requests for bids requiring vendors and suppliers to provide information on the environmental qualities of their products.
- Monitor on an annual basis the progress in evaluating and selecting sustainable products.

Table 5.1 Methods of Campus Source Reduction and Reuse (RIS, 1991)

Method	Description
Purchase durable, standardized, repairable and reusable products	Waste generation can be avoided if a college considers the life cycle and reusability of products purchased. Consideration should be given to durable design, ease of repair (in terms of simplicity and replacement parts), and reusability. Additionally, products should be easily recycled once once their useful life ends.
Reduce food waste generation	Food waste can be a significant portion of a university waste stream. Methods of purchasing food can be modified to minimize waste. For example, a per pound or per item assessment can be utilized at some food service establishments rather than an all-you-can-eat dining hall meal ticket.
Reduce and reuse landscape waste	Leaving landscape waste in place-particularly grass-is a very effective method of waste reduction which is already commonly practiced on campuses throughout Illinois. Additionally, woody materials can be ground and used as cover in landscaping.
Promote duplex document copying	Modify copy machine procurement guidelines to obtain duplex capable copying machines, and develop campus policy of duplexing for documents of multiple pages. Charge less per copy at public photocopiers when the duplexing option is chosen.
Reduce the junk mail sent to campus	Junk mail-mail that is mass distributed at reduced postal rates and includes catalogs, advertisements, and solicitations-is often never read and can burden the university postal system. Removing one's name from the mailing list is often as simple as writing to an address and indicating such. Write to: Direct Marketing Association, Mail Preference Services, 11 West 42nd Street, PO Box 3861, New York, NY 10163.
Reduce junk mail generated on campus	On colleges there are large volume of campus communications. Methods to avoid paper redundancy (e.g., kiosks) can impact waste generation on campus.
Increase e-mail and voice mail use	Colleges can lessen paper generation by using campus computer and telephone systems for electronic mail (e-mail) and voice mail. Initiating training sessions for staff and faculty on such use is an essential step.
Avoid purchase of disposables in kitchens, cafeterias, and offices	If used, disposable beverage containers and dinnerware represent a sizable portion of the waste stream from food service operations. Replacing disposables with flatware, china, and glassware can reduce waste stream amounts.

Table 5.1 (cont.)

Method	Description
Provide incentives to use reusables	Offer cash discounts on food and beverages purchased with reusable flatware, china, and glassware. Provide reusable glasses for purchase by student, staff and faculty, and offer cash discounts on refills.
Operate an on-campus waste exchange	One department's waste may be another's needed products. A waste exchange is a listing of products or an actual storage area for products which may be reused. Items can include used furniture, office supplies, computer equipment, scientific equipment, boxes, packaging materials, or surplus equipment.
Reuse or remanufacture wooden shipping pallets	Wood pallets used for regular truckload product delivery to college campuses create a bulky waste stream item, making their disposal awkward. Instead, pallets may be reused for storage on campus, remanufactured into new pallets, or burned as boiler fuel.
Reuse student furniture and dorm room loft wood	Sleeping lofts, sofas, upholstered chairs, and other furniture not owned by the university are often found in student rooms. At the end of the academic year, students often have little opportunity to save or sell these materials and may leave it behind. A sales and storage program which offers a place to store such materials over summer break is one way to bridge the gap to reuse.
Sponsor collection of clothing, books and appliances for reuse	Students frequently have clothing, appliances, and other items which they choose not to take home when the term ends. These items can be collected as part of a standard charity/recycling program for reuse elsewhere.
Reuse/remanufacture laserwriter toner cartridges	Toner cartridges can be reinked or remanufactured for a longer useful life. A convenient method of reusing cartridges would be for the primary procurement agency on campus to offer cartridge recycling service and offer a discount with old cartridges returned.
Reuse boxes, envelopes and packing materials	Packing materials can be saved for reuse. Reuse campus mail envelopes for circulation.
Use food service buckets as collection containers	5 gallon plastic buckets used in bulk food and other services are appropriate for use as recycling containers and can defray capital costs of purchasing recycling containers.

- Adopt a model purchasing policy for sustainable development that incorporates the above recommendations, as well as standards and implementation activities

5.2 Recycling

Regardless of the location or material type, there are three fundamental components to recycling: collection, processing, and marketing. Buyers/market sources of recyclable materials for Illinois and surrounding states are discussed in Chapter 4. Collection and/or processing are activities performed by a college staff or contractor. Two methods are typically used for collection and processing of recyclables: i) Collection of recyclables separated from the normal refuse stream at the source (termed source separation recycling), followed by minimal processing (i.e., contaminant removal and subsequent material categorization); ii) Collection of recyclables with the normal refuse stream followed by more extensive processing (i.e., manual and/or automated sorting of recyclables from mixed waste).

As shown in Chapter 3 and Table 5.2, waste stream components recycled at colleges typically are generated according to specific functions within the college. As such, a college recycling program should be designed with this in mind. General areas (e.g., student unions) and housing facilities generate recyclables which most closely resembles that of a typical municipal recycling program; office and academic areas are almost entirely

Table 5.2 Materials Recycled at Colleges Based on Facility Type

Recyclable Material	General Areas	Office/ Academic	Food Service	Dormitory/ Housing	Central Stores
Aluminum/metal beverage containers	•	•		•	
Food waste			•		
Glass food and beverage containers	•		•	•	
HDPE beverage and food containers			•	•	
Paper Products					
Corrugated cardboard/paperboard	•	•	•	•	•
High grade office paper					
Computer printout paper	•	•		•	•
White bond/ledger paper	•	•		•	•
Assorted colored bond/ledger paper		•			
Low grade office paper (mixed paper)	•	•		•	•
Newsprint	•			•	
PET beverage containers				•	
Tin (steel) beverage and food containers	•		•		

varying grades of paper; and food service is comprised of bulk packaging materials. These individual programs are largely dependent on different target audiences as well. For office and academic areas, faculty, staff and students are the target group; for food service, the food service staff will have the most impact (food service customers will also have a large impact if source separation is utilized); and for general areas and dormitory recycling students, housekeeping, and janitorial staff will have the most impact.

5.2.1 Implementation Steps

A number of steps need to be taken in initiating a recycling program. As campus size grows, so does the importance of each step. As an example, Table 5.3 shows the implementation steps (not necessarily in chronological order) as applied to setting up a campus recycling program at Cornell University. The Cornell implementation occurred in four main phases over an 8 month period.

5.2.2 Model Department Recycling Policy

A few simple, departmental policy steps should be set for both waste generators and service staff to assist in recycling implementation. There are also steps which departmental managers can take to promote recycling activities. These steps are reviewed as follows (Marks, 1990):

Generators/Staff Steps:
- College departments/divisions and offices should participate in recycling programs as they become available.
- All such groups should develop internal programs for waste diversion.
- College service staff should be recognized for their role in handling recyclables.
- Existing recycling efforts for materials above and beyond those collected and marketed by the college should be recognized.

Managerial Steps:
- Departmental managers should demonstrate full support to the recycling program by committing the human, communication and financial resources needed to encourage high levels of participation.
- Departmental managers should, with the assistance of the recycling office and purchasing department, explore reduction and reuse strategies to reduce the flow of solid waste from the department.
- Support recycling and reduction by participating yourself.
- Use staff meetings to clarify expectations of staff to participate.
- Ensure that departmental policy, procedure, and purchasing habits support recycling and reduction.
- Provide inter-departmental communication.
- Using cost-avoidance, establish a financially self-supporting program goal.

Table 5.3 Implementation Steps for Cornell University Recycling Program (Hargett and Osborn, 1989)

Step	Description
1. Announcement by Senior Administration	A letter of introduction of the new recycling program was sent to all of Cornell's employees by the provost and senior vice president. The announcement introduced "Cornell Recycles" to the university and asked employees to be prepared to for the introduction of the program to individual buildings. The letter also outlined how the program would operate, what would be expected of employees, and solicited their cooperation.
2. Purchase of Equipment	Equipment was needed for an initial 9,000 staff and 130 buildings. A plan was established to purchase the equipment in installments. Bids were obtained for the total quantity of each item, and purchase contracts were awarded based on the total quantities required. The items listed below were purchased over the course of 8 months during main implementation of the program: • 12,000 small trash containers • 500 32 gallon trash containers with dollies • 130 1 1/2 yd3 tilt truck dumpsters with lids • 50,000 33 gallon clear trash can liners (initial order) • 15,000 small container liners • 30,000 labels: 'Recyclable Paper' and 'Non-Recyclables' • 250 large dumpster labels: 'Cornell Recycles'
3. Contract Established with Vendor	Cornell entered into a limited-term contract with the vendor for its services. The contract included terms and conditions regarding the pickup and payment to the university for all campus mixed recyclable paper.
4. Orientation of Custodial Managers	Early in the planning process, meetings were held with custodial management staff. The important sessions were of particular assistance in reviewing and fine tuning the actual collection mechanics for the program. Decisions were made about which buildings would be brought on-line first and serve as examples for all other buildings. Equipment planning was performed for each building on a individual basis. An active dialogue was maintained with custodial mangers throughout the nine-month implementation period.

Table 5.3 (Cont.)

Step	Description
5. Orientation of Custodial Staff	Meetings were held with all custodial staff in each building as it was brought on line. Considerable emphasis was placed on these sessions to thoroughly familiarize the staff with the mechanics of the process. The importance of the recycling program and the role that they individually and collectively would play in the process were discussed. These sessions proved to be extremely productive in that many practical ideas were generated regarding the actual engineering of the collection process. For example, the suggestion that recyclable paper would be collected in clear plastic bags versus black bags for ordinary trash came out of this process.
6. Initial Building Contact, Promotion and Setup	Building coordinators for each facility were contacted in advance of each planned setup. The recycling program was reviewed in detail and promotional material provided for distribution to all building employees. This material included an introductory letter and a list of the most frequently asked questions about the program. Immediately following its distribution, the buildings were setup for recycling by the custodial staff. Setups were usually performed on Saturday, and the buildings were ready for recycling the following Monday. Close contact was maintained with building coordinators and custodial staff as each individual step was performed.
7. Monitoring the Program	The program directors view the process of monitoring and followup to be essential to the success of the program. An active dialogue continues with building coordinators and the custodial staff throughout the campus. Continued feedback has aided the program with excellent suggestions for improvements in the program design and actual hands-on operation.

5.2.3 Source Separation College Recycling

For most colleges with recycling activities, source separation collection is commonly used. The most commonly employed method is containerized collection at central locations inside and/or outside each building. Generators (office workers, faculty, housing residents) separate recyclables from refuse using recycling collection containers. In an office or desk setting, one container per sort (such as an office paper container) is typically used. Dormitory and housing residents typically collect materials commingled in a single container and then perform a 2, 3, or 4 component sort upon emptying. The containers are then transported to central collection containers by the generator or custodial staff. Central collection containers are either emptied on-location with a refuse collection vehicle or interchanged with an empty container and transported to a processing facility. Processing includes additional sortation and removal of contaminants to an acceptable level, and densification for transport to market.

5.2.3.1 Container Selection

Because the source separation method establishes a separate path for recyclables, it is necessary to add a separate container collection system. The addition of a new system of collection containers is one of the primary capital cost components in establishing a campus recycling program. There are four levels of container collection: i) office/dwelling unit based 'personal' collection containers; ii) central collection containers from an aggregate of personal containers; iii) campus grounds collection containers and iv) processing containers for use prior to/following processing. Personal collection containers may be anything from a cardboard box or 5 gallon bucket to a 22 gallon recycling bin. A central collection container may be any type container dedicated to recycling service. Examples include 30-90 gallon wheeled containers for inside buildings and 55 gallon drums, yard boxes (dumpsters), or 20-30 yd^3 roll-off boxes located outside of buildings. Considerations for containers and labeling include:

- Containers must be approved by the local safety and fire marshall.

- Containers must be equipped with a closure to minimize water acceptance and fire risk.

- Building containers should be wheelable at the maximum capacity load possible.

- Signs designating which container(s) are to be used for each recyclable should be coordinated with the container (e.g., by color or shape) to eliminate confusion caused by same color containers. Signs should be large, legible, and ideally at eye level.

- Containers should be uniform, attractive, convenient, well labeled and visibly different from refuse containers.

- Material designation signs should be affixed to container sidewalls (not nearby building walls or removable covers) and specify what is unacceptable as well as acceptable.

5.2.3.2 Container Site Selection

When siting central collection containers the following should be considered:

- A standard location protocol should be followed where possible throughout the campus (e.g., on every floor of a building by the staircase, and in the rear of every building).

- Containers must be located such that they are convenient to use for the staff and/or students.

- Containers must be located such that they are convenient for collection by the custodial staff. Loading, transporting, and emptying should be as simple as possible so as to minimize staff hours expended.

- Site selection for recycling containers and storage areas should be approved by the custodial supervisor, fire marshall and safety office, in addition to the recycling coordinator.

- Containers should be located at all buildings throughout a college campus to confirm recycling as a university-wide college effort.

5.2.4 Custodial Partnership

Utilizing the expertise and resources of the campus custodial department to perform in-building recycling collection duties can have a number of positive outcomes to a college recycling program. Campus custodial staff can help recycling by providing: i) expertise with regards to waste flow in individual buildings; ii) optimal placement of central collection containers and building recycling dumpsters; iii) a built-in system of waste handling into which recycling can be relatively easily incorporated; iv) daily monitoring of contamination and its source; v) Early identification of problem areas, and vi) consistent service. A typical time estimate for custodial involvement in office paper collection is 15 minutes/day for emptying central hallway containers and 30 seconds/office container/day (Potter, 1990).

The University of Minnesota has retained the support of the custodial department for its source separation recycling program. To assure consistent communication with and within the custodial department, a custodial working group was established. The group meets three to four times per year and is comprised of custodial principals, supervisors, crew members and representatives from the recycling program. It is important to include individuals who are both supportive and non-supportive of recycling to get all viewpoints of how recycling affects custodial duties. Such a group could serve to vent frustrations, suggest improvements, and indicate what does/does not work.

5.2.5 Mixed Waste Collection College Recycling

Mixed waste collection in conjunction with centralized processing and removal of recyclables is a practice seldom utilized at colleges. In fact, the only college which routinely performs such processing is the University of California-Los Angeles. The UCLA program, a hybrid of source separation recycling and mixed waste processing, is designed to be non-intrusive in nature (the opposite of what most recycling campaigns are intended to be) but in the first full year of operation (1990) achieved a 60% landfill diversion. The program's primary goals are:

- Divert the maximum amount of waste from landfills.

- Minimize impact on the campus' continuing operations and programs.

- Institutionalize the program by integrating it into the ongoing waste management program and by making it economically self-sufficient.

To perform an initial "selective" separation of mostly recyclable from mostly non-recyclable refuse, three separate collection routes, based on the general waste characteristics of each particular building, were established: i) commingled mixed paper and other recyclables, ii) standard refuse, and iii) landscape waste. Buildings whose refuse is predominantly paper are part of the mixed paper collection route (Route i). This includes facilities such as classrooms, offices, libraries, and computer centers. Because all waste is processed, users of these buildings are not equipped with individual recycling containers and there is no in-building recycling. Buildings whose refuse may be questionable (i.e., potentially hazardous to process) or all-together not easily recycled are part of the standard refuse (Route ii). This includes science-related buildings, physical plants, maintenance facilities, or food service areas. Landscape waste routes are situated in accordance with area landscaping (Route iii).

While mixed waste processing is the primary recycling method used, a limited amount of source separation is performed throughout the UCLA campus. Waste generating buildings which are on the refuse route (Route ii) who wish to be part of the recycling program are supplied with mixed paper route dumpsters upon request. However, the individual users in such facilities are required to source separate paper generated and dispose of it in the appropriate dumpster without the assistance of custodial staff. Student housing facilities are serviced by Routes (i) and (ii) above, and as such, students perform source separation and are provided with central collection containers for commingled recyclables on each floor. Student housing source separates all grades of paper, corrugated cardboard, beverage cans, plastics and glass.

Because of their size and bulk, mixed metals and wood products are also source separated from the main waste stream on a call basis.

5.3 Processing of Recyclables

Because paper is the primary constituent of a college waste stream and because no automated method exists for sortation of varying grades of paper, manual sortation is the method primarily used in colleges for processing of recyclables. Manual sortation can range from sifting through collection containers or piles dumped on a warehouse floor to conveyor belt processing with an appropriate number of picking stations. The former is obviously crude, with a low capital but high operating expense, while the latter is a higher capital but lower operating expense. A conveyor belt pick system may be used for sorting any number of waste stream components desired. With source separation recycling it is preferable to minimize the processing. A number of publications exist which routinely examine the tradeoffs between source separation and commingled collection recycling (Resource Recycling, Biocycle, and Recycling Today, to name a few). These publications also examine methods for recyclables processing and preparation for shipment, and periodically issue manufacturer directories for sortation, baling and processing equipment.

Varying levels of automated sortation (and capital costs) exist for recyclables: magnetic separation for removal of ferrous metals; eddy current separation for removal of non-ferrous metals; weight based separation for removal of plastics; x-ray fluorescence for removal of PVC plastics from plastic streams; optical recognition of colored glass. These recyclables comprise a small portion of college waste streams. These processing steps are unlikely to be cost effective.

A college must evaluate the campus waste generation rate and cost of waste disposal against the cost of processing equipment or contractor processing and determine if on-campus waste processing is feasible. For smaller colleges (e.g., community colleges) it simply may be more appropriate to limit types of recyclables collected (e.g., only high grade white office paper) rather than recycle all paper and have to bear the cost of processing. On the other hand, colleges have ready work forces available to process recyclables.

5.4 Recycling Based on Facility Function

5.4.1 Academic and Office Areas

Two recycling methods are typically used for office and academic areas: custodial-waste basket collection, and employee-central container collection. In the latter, staff are provided with personal, small containers (5 gallons or less) for accumulation of paper; larger containers (30-90 gallon) are made available throughout buildings for users to empty personal containers. Custodians or dedicated recycling staff empty central collection container contents into recycling dumpsters located outside buildings, or exchange full containers with empty containers and provide transport to the processing center. With custodial-waste basket collection, custodial staff provide the service of emptying personal paper collection containers and subsequent transport to central containers.

Refer to Appendix D for a listing of additional guidebooks for planning office and other recycling activities.

5.4.2 Housing and Residence Halls

Housing and residence hall recycling requires a greater number of central collection containers outside and throughout the building for the many types of recyclables (Figure 5.1) found in this environment. Since an increased number of outdoor containers is necessary (a higher cost), establishment of collection points which conveniently serve two or more buildings should be considered. Components typically collected at college residence halls resemble curbside recycling: newsprint, computer printout and high grade office paper, glass, metals, plastics, and magazines.

5.4.3 Food Service Recycling

Food waste is one component of the waste stream often landfilled. If diverted from ultimate disposal, food waste can have a significant impact on recycling levels. For the years 1988-1990, Rutgers University recovered an average 1100 tons/year of food waste, 43% by weight of all recyclables recovered. Soiled plates are brought by students and staff to the dishwashing area adjacent to each dining center. Dining staff scrape food waste into a pulper similar to a garbage disposal. The dining service food waste is ground, excess liquid is removed with a centrifuge and discharged, and residuals are placed in 55 gallon barrels which are stored in a walk-in cooler. Barrels are picked up by farmers at a university cost of $5/barrel for use as cattle feed. To encourage reuse of food waste, the state of New Jersey has compiled a list of farmers who will accept food waste for livestock feed.

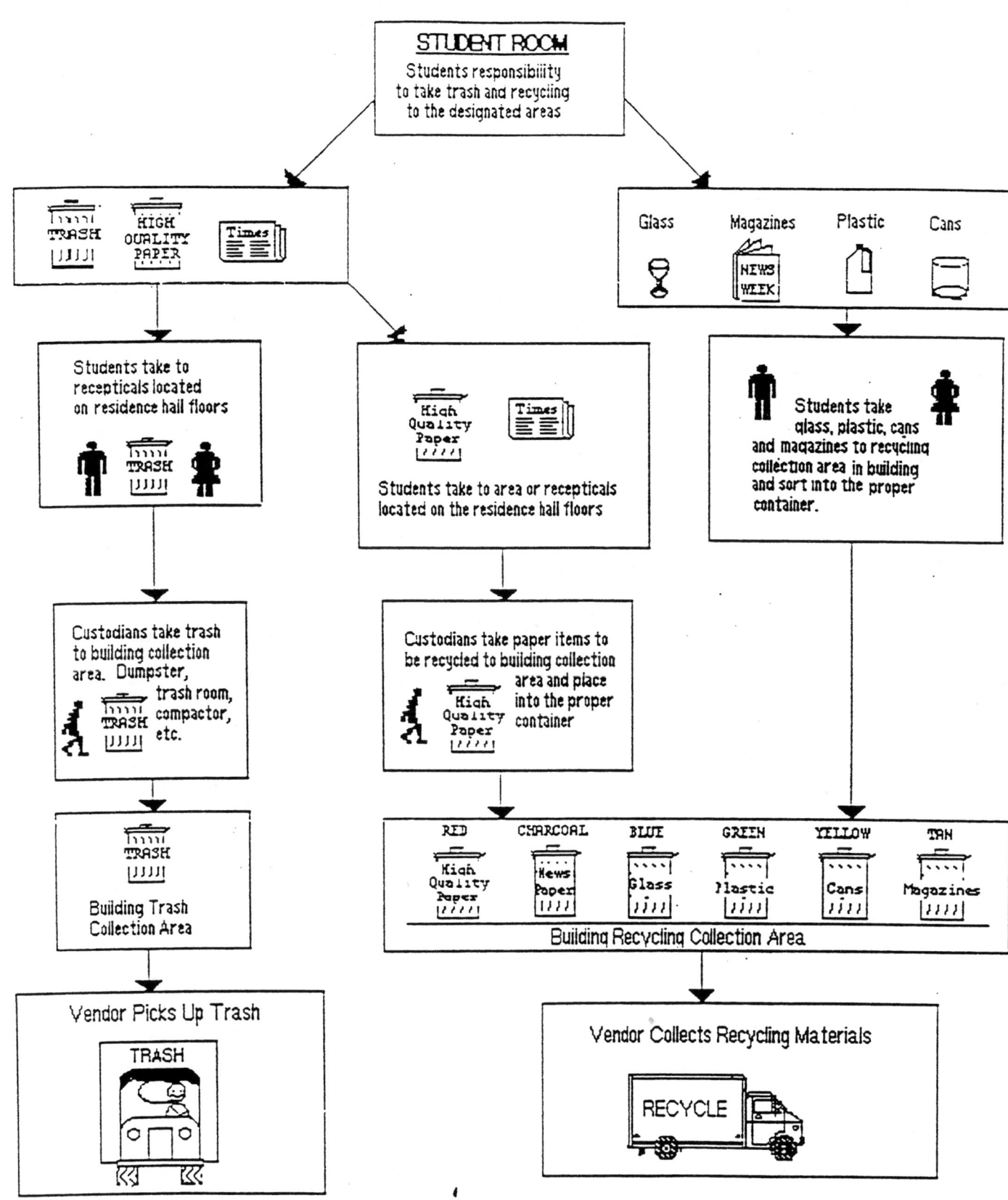

Figure 5.1 Cornell University Residence Hall Source Separation Arrangement

Additionally, each dining facility is equipped with a small size baler for cardboard and a non-recyclable compactor. Glass, plastic and steel food service containers are kept separated. Since the dining facility staff handles both trash and recyclables in a very defined area, recycling was simple to implement. It is estimated that 75% of Rutgers' dining service waste is diverted from ultimate disposal.

The National Association of College and University Food Services has established a food service waste recycling network, whereby contacts can be made and ideas exchanged. The association may be reached at NACUFS, 1405 S. Harrison Rd. Suite 303, East Lansing, MI, 48824, (517) 332-2494.

Please note that Illinois law (PA76-227) prohibits the feeding of raw garbage to swine or to other animals or poultry on farms where swine are present.

5.4.4 Surplus Equipment & Scrap Recycling

One method of recycling equipment no longer used is to establish a cooperative of surplus equipment, where such materials can be marketed for resale within or outside the university. Since much surplus equipment is bulky, an on-call pickup service can be utilized for such a program. The University of British Columbia has established a surplus equipment recycling facility (SERF) program for this purpose. In 1990 approximately 2600 pieces of equipment were sold externally and 1040 pieces were sold internally. Gross annual sales were $228,900 and $35,190, respectively (UBC, 1991). Since scrap metal is also typically bulky and weighty, it may also be collected on a call basis.

5.4.5 Chemical Redistribution

A simple method of minimizing hazardous and special waste generation due to chemicals is a chemical redistribution program. Since college safety departments are typically responsible for intra-university transport of chemicals, a chemical redistribution program would be simple to implement. Under such a program, any college department can receive, free of charge, excess pre-owned chemicals. The safety department could also publish a periodic inventory of available chemicals for faculty information. The University of Illinois-Urbana has established a chemical redistribution program for bulk solvents, agricultural chemicals, and laboratory reagents which are usually abandoned, obsolete, or otherwise unwanted because research staff have overpurchased, relocated, or changed research emphasis.

5.5 Education and Promotion

A number of educational and promotional methods have been utilized to increase rates and quality of recycled materials collected. Educational materials such as posters, brochures, flyers, newsletters, and newspaper advertisements and articles should be frequent and exhibit a high level of quality. Recycling instructions should be clear and to the point. Information should be provided with regard to where recycled materials go and what they are made into. Posted information should have a consistent theme across all buildings and be readily identifiable. Each building should have visible listings of where its recycling bins are located. As a minimum, the following education methods should be utilized upon implementation of a recycling program:

- Message from the college president
- Newspaper articles
- Advertisements in campus newspapers
- Letters to faculty, staff and students
- Notice to housing residents
- Distribution of recycling instructions
- Identification of recycling locations
- Posters and signage.

Additionally, an overall program theme can serve to coordinate campus involvement. It will promote visibility and tie together separated recycling activities. Simple, clear logos and slogans are typically used.

A simple way of increasing awareness is to establish a building recycling coordinator for each facility. Such a person could serve as a source of information to others, arrange for special pickups, assist in reducing the confusion of recycling, and arrange for deliveries of additional recycling containers.

6. Recycling Implementation at Colleges

6.1 Cost Elements to Consider in College Recycling

The size of a campus, number of buildings, total number of students/staff/faculty, materials collected, and level of processing are all factors that affect program cost. When evaluating type and options for college recycling/waste reduction, the following cost components should be considered:

Capital Costs
- Collection
    - Personal Office Containers
    - Residence Hall Recycling Bins
    - Central Area Recycling Containers
    - Building Dumpsters
    - General Campus Recycling Containers
- Transport
    - Recycling/Transport Vehicles
    - Refuse Packers
- Processing
    - Facility Construction
    - Storage Areas for Processed/Unprocessed Goods
    - Conveyor Belt/Semi-Automated Processing and Feed Equipment
    - Balers, Glass Crushers, Granulators, Densifiers, etc.
- Recycling Education and Promotion
    - Container Labeling
    - Campus Notification
    - Information Packet Handout

Annual Costs
- Administrative
- Collection
    - Container Replacement
- Processing
    - Building Operation and Maintenance
    - Baler/Processing Equipment Operation and Maintenance
- Transport
    - Vehicle Operation and Maintenance
- Labor
    - Recycling Coordinator
    - Janitorial Staff Modification
    - Collection and Processing Staff
    - Staff Training
- Recycling Education and Promotion
    - Promotional Advertisements
    - Continued Campus Education
    - New Student/Staff Recycling Orientation
- Expansion Costs

6.2 Estimating College Recycling Costs

6.2.1 Actual Costs

Actual recycling costs from fully implemented recycling programs are hard to come by. Because recycling at colleges is often integrated into the overall waste management budget, identifying the net cost or profit due to recycling only is difficult. Compounding the problem are factors such as insufficient recordkeeping of waste reduction measures, and only partially implemented programs. The latter can give recycling an extremely expensive appearance.

Some campuses have independently monitored the costs of their recycling program. A summary of program costs, materials collected and collection methods are shown in Table 6.1. The generally accepted method for evaluating the net cost of recycling is: Net Program Cost = Actual Program Cost - Revenues of Recyclables - Avoided Collection and Disposal Costs. Because recyclable material prices and landfill tip fees vary widely, the cost data shown in Table 6.1 is actual program cost without crediting due to income from grants, recycled materials revenues, or landfill diversion. The annual costs shown are largely for campuses in later stages of implementation (i.e., campus wide, all materials targeted), and do include some capital startup expenditures. Because each college conducts its own brand of recycling and cost accounting, emphasis should be given to the schools shown as examples of recycling costs rather than between-schools comparative costs, e.g., each school is in a different stage of implementation and has its own unique program, and therefore the costs shown are not comparable. It is not known whether the schools shown included _all_ cost aspects of recycling (e.g., the additional cost of janitorial staff collecting office paper at deskside).

6.2.2 Startup Cost Estimates

Startup cost estimates are naturally performed for college recycling programs prior to implementation. Such numbers are also easier to come by than actual costs. However, because they are only estimates, they should be considered with caution. As indicated above, the costs shown below do not include avoided collection and disposal costs or recyclables revenue.

The 1990 projected operating costs for office paper and residence hall recycling implementation at Northwestern University (student population=9,000) were as follows:

Table 6.1   Summary of Campus Recycling Costs

Component	U. Illinois Urbana	U. Minnesota Minneapolis	U. Michigan Ann Arbor
Year Reported	Fiscal 1991	Annual 1989	Fiscal 1990
Materials Recycled			
Glass	•	•	•
Metal Beverage	•	•	•
Metals (scrap form)	•	•	•
Paper			
Corrugated Cardboard	•	•	•
Newsprint	•	•	•
Magazines	somewhat		
White/Computer paper	•	•	•
Mixed	somewhat		•
Yard Waste	•	•	•
Plastics			
HDPE Beverage	•		•
PET Beverage	•		
Quantities Recycled (tons)			
Beverage Cans	18	5	6
Cardboard	381	397	333
Glass	48	13	a
Metals	437	14	0
Paper	731	708	748
Plastics	3	0	0
Wood/Brush/Yard Waste	710	186	223
Other	0	223	96
Total Tonnage	2,328	1,546	1,406
Recycling Method	Source separation-commingled paper container switch method	Source separation container switch method	Source separation
Processing	Off-Site	On-Site	Off-site
Costs ($)			
Labor	58,500	164,604	na
Equipment	52,500	43,861	na
Promotion	5,300	991	na
Processing	95,300	20,218	na
Other	5,400	23,492	na
Total	$217,000	$253,166	$392,271
Cost ($/ton)	$93	$164	$279
Cost, excl. wood [b]	$134	$186	$332

a. Included with beverage cans.
b. Wood/brush/yard waste often comprises a large weight fraction but a small cost fraction; therefore excluding it may give a more realistic estimate of recycling cost.

Annual Operating Costs	
Recycling Director	35,000
Benefits	6,475
Student Labor; 80 hrs/wk • 52 wk/year • $15/hr	62,400
Supplies	8,000
Annual Operating Costs (cont.)	
Promotion	1,000
Other	800
Subtotal	$113,675

The initial <u>projected startup</u> costs for office paper and residence hall recycling implementation at Northwestern University were:

One Time Startup Expenses	
Consultant Evaluation and Optimization	12,000
Dining Area Containers; 120 • $45 each	5,400
Containers at Vending Machines; 80 • $55 each	4,400
Containers for Dormitories	
Fiber drums in Refuse Rooms; 240 • $15 each	3,600
Loading Dock Steel Drums; 180 • $10 each	1,800
High Grade Office Paper Containers; 320 • $40 each	12,800
Desk Paper Boxes; 3,500 • $1.25 each	4,375
Office Equipment, Computer	6,000
Other	10,000
Subtotal	$60,375
Year 1 Total	$174,050
(Source NU, 1990)	

The above costs do not include charges for hauling, or processing. For comparison, Northwestern's 1989 refuse disposal bill totaled $670,000 (5,750 tons), not including cost of custodial staff labor, administrative overhead, or fleet maintenance.

The University of Illinois Urbana-Champaign (UIUC, student population=38,000) is phasing in its recycling program over a five year period. The materials it collects is shown in Table 6.1. Its five year <u>projected</u> startup and operating costs for campus-wide and residence hall recycling implementation are shown in Table 6.2. Once again, the estimates shown do not include charges for hauling, marketing or processing recyclables (the original intent being that revenues generated from recyclables would offset processing

Table 6.2 University of Illinois Five Year Recycling Implementation Budget (UIUC, 1989, 1990, 1991)

Cost Component	Budgeted Fiscal Year[a] Expenditures for Phase-In ($)						
	1989	1990	1991	1992	1993	5 Year Total	1994 [b]
Labor							
Recycling Coordinators	37,500	62,900	64,900	69,300	72700	307,300	76,300
Student Labor	8,400	7,200	8,200	8,200	9,200	41,200	10,200
Travel / Seminars	2,250	2,500	2,500	2,500	3,000	12,750	3,000
Office Equipment, Supplies	2,500	1,500	1,500	1,500	1,500	8,500	1,500
Promotion	5,750	6,750	7,500	7,300	8,500	35,800	8,400
Office Containers	7,500	10,500	11,000	11,600	12,200	52,800	4,200
Dormitory Containers	10,000	5,000	2,500	2,500	5,000	25,000	2,500
Collection Barrels	11,250	15,750	16,500	17,400	18,200	79,100	4,200
Load Luggers	11,000	11,800	9,600	7,500	7,800	47,700	2,600
Residence Hall Promotion	20,000	20,000	15,000	7,500	5,000	67,500	5,000
Total	116,150	143,900	139,200	135,300	143,100	677,650	117,900
Actual Expenditures ($)	47,000	154,000	217,000				
Total Mat. Diverted (tons)	200	1,614	2,328				
Total MSW Landfilled (yd^3)	61,000	48,000	46,000				
Landfill Cost ($)	291,000	336,000	447,000				

a. July 1 - June 30
b. Estimated operating expenditures after the 5 year phase-in is shown in the fiscal year 1994 column.

costs). Actual expenditures are also shown in Table 6.2. The <u>actual average</u> cost per student at UIUC for the first three years of the implementation plan was $3.67/student /year for general, academic, and residence hall recycling. The cost overruns were due in part to a $10,000 and $40,000 payment in 1990 and 1991, respectively, to the local recycling center to assist in the cost of collection and processing. The estimated operating expenditures after the 5 year phase-in is shown in the fiscal year 1994 column.

6.3   Exemplary College Recycling

6.3.1 Aggressive University Recycling Programs

The colleges shown in Table 6.3 have established aggressive recycling/waste diversion programs. Source separation recycling rates range from 11% to 34% by weight. The recovery of food waste or mixed paper have the largest effect on the diversion rate for source separation type programs. Other items recycled by the above programs which are not listed in Table 6.3 include clothing, furniture, and expanded polystyrene.

The recycling rates shown are yearly values on a mass basis and therefore do not reflect efforts of waste minimization which may have occurred over a number of years. Percentages by weight are given to avoid confusion resulting from varying densities and compaction rates. For example, even though the University of Illinois-Urbana shows a diversion level of 15% (weight basis) for Fiscal Year 91, it reports a reduction of 44% (volumetric basis) from FY 87 (82,000 yd^3 landfilled) through FY 91 (46,000 yd^3 landfilled; Hoss, 1991). The effect of volumetric versus weight based measurement is readily evident in this example. Since waste diversion through recycling and procurement reduction are measured on a weight basis, and because landfill disposed refuse is always compacted, thereby ensuring a uniform density, waste diversion rates should be measured on a weight basis.

UCLA has a high diversion rate because its low-paper content non-recyclable waste stream (37% of all waste generated) is diverted to a waste-to-energy facility; the high paper content waste stream (45% of all waste) is separated/processed at a transfer station, and another 5% is source separated.

Table 6.3   Aggressive University Recycling Programs

	OCC[a]	ONP[a]	Office Ledger	Mixed Paper	Glass	Beverage Cans	Scrap Metal	Yard Waste	Wood Waste	Food Waste	Batteries	Used Oil	Demo Debris	Diversion Rate (wt%)
Source Separation Recycling														
Dartmouth College W. Hochstin, Housekeeping Dept Dartmouth College, McKenzie Hall Hanover, NH 03755	•	•	•	•	•	•	•	•	•	•	•	•		22%
Northwestern University K. Huber, Physical Plant 2020 Ridge Avenue, Evanston, IL 60208	•	•	•	•	•	•	•	•	•					11%
Rugers University R. Ching, Facilities Maintenance PO Box 5074, New Brunswick, NJ 08903-5074	•	•	•	•	•	•	•	•	•	•		•		34%
University of Colorado J. DeBell UMC 331A Campus Box 207 Boulder, CO 80309	•	•	•	•	•	•	•	•	•			•		20%
University of Illinois-Urbana T. Hoss, Recycling and Materials Reduction 1501 S. Oak St., Champaign, IL 61820	•	•	•	•	•	•	•	•	•				•	15%
University of Michigan J. Marks, Plant Grounds & Services 326 East Hoover, Ann Arbor, MI 48109-1002	•	•	•	•	•	•	•	•	•		•		•	14%
University of Minnesota D. Donatucci, Physical Plant Operations 3001 Fairmont St. SE, Minneapolis, MN 55514	•	•	•	•	•	•	•	•	•			•	•	17%
Mixed Waste Processing														
University of California Los Angeles E.J. Kirby, Facilities Management 711 Circle South Drive, Los Angeles, CA 90024	•	•	•	•	•	•	•	•	•			•	•	60%

a. Old corrugated cardboard (OCC); Old Newsprint (ONP).

6.3.2 Guidance Reports

A number of studies with subsequent reports were reviewed from colleges for the purposes of this guidebook. There are a few which were quite thorough undertakings and may serve as excellent examples in planning a recycling program. Recommended college solid waste reports are as follows:

School	Title	Source	Price
Univ. Washington at Seattle	Waste Stream Analysis Phase 1: Solid Waste Minimization & Management Study	L. Bender, CCA Inc. 1001 4th Ave, Suite 2722 Seattle, WA. 98154-1107	$8
Dartmouth College	Reduce, Recycle, and Educate: A Solid Waste Management Program for Dartmouth College	W. Hochstin, Director Dartmouth Recycles Dartmouth College Hanover, NH 03755	$5
Univ. Michigan at Ann Arbor	The Sourcebook on Solid Waste Management at the Univ. of Michigan	J. Marks, Coordinator Plant Grounds and Waste Management Dept. Univ. Michigan 362 E. Hoover Ann Arbor, MI 48109-1002	N/A
Univ. British Columbia	Building A Sustainable Community: An Integrated Solid Waste Management Programme Planning Element	P. Nault University of British Columbia Dept. Plant Operations 2210 West Mall Vancouver, BC V6T 1Z4	N/A
Univ. Illinois Urbana-Champaign	Campus-Wide Recycling Report and Recommendations to the Vice-Chancellor for Administrative Affairs	T. Hoss University of Illinois-UC Physical Plant Svc. Bldg. 1501 S. Oak St. Champaign, IL 61820	$10

7. Recycled Content Product Procurement

The College Recycling Law requires identification of frequently purchased products with recycled content and a policy dictum that recycled content materials be preferred over "virgin" content materials, assuming specifications are satisfied. A college procurement system affects solid waste disposal in two ways: i) the quantity and/or types of products procured are a direct input to college waste generation; ii) the recycled material composition of products procured can lessen demand of similar "virgin" material products and increase demand for materials recovered in a recycling program. Methods to modify procurement in order to reduce waste generation (Item i) are discussed in Chapter 4. The purpose of this chapter is to provide guidance on purchasing products with recycled content.

7.1 Procurement Policy Elements

Implicit in this aspect of the college recycling law is the necessary commitment that colleges will purchase products with recycled material content when such products compare favorably in terms of conformance to specifications, cost, and availability to products with non-recycled content (virgin products).

A number of steps may be performed to encourage procurement of recycled content products. First, inventory the type and consumption rate of goods on-campus for which recycled content materials are available, and identify producers of such recycled content goods. For colleges, paper products and their recycled content would naturally comprise a majority of this evaluation. Next, a cost analysis of purchasing virgin versus recycled products should be performed and weighed against normal purchasing requirements (i.e., conformance to specifications, availability, shipping, recycled content, and durability). Third, it is recommended that new products be tested with major campus users for acceptability. Fourth, the evaluation of a different pricing structure for recycled content versus virgin products should be investigated. A price preference to support the purchase of recycled content products may be possible. Lastly, a system to monitor the progress of recycled product procurement should be developed. Such monitoring should be included in annual recycling/waste management reports.

Once acceptable recycled content products are identified, purchasing departments can communicate their recycling policy to other school departments and encourage it as standard policy. Campus media services may be utilized to regularly update the campus community on the availability and performance of recycled content products. Proven products should be used in highly visible applications. For example, department letterhead can be printed on recycled content paper and recycled content copier paper used at copy machines. Also, special advertising of stocked recycled content products can be conducted.

7.2 Design for Recycling

It is also important to consider a college's recycling activities during procurement modification. Purchase and produce (e.g., publish) products which are acceptable in the university's recycling programs. For example, if a department is involved in producing publications, design the publications such that when obsolete, they may be recycled in the college's paper recycling program. The following recyclability criteria for publications have been developed at the University of Michigan (Marks, 1990):

- Use stapled or water soluble bindings over hot-melt bindings.

- Select white ledger or other paper amenable to recycling over groundwood paper.

- Use non-glossy covers for publications rather than glossy covers.

- Do not use polymer coated papers.

- Avoid heavy inking in bold colors.

7.3 Specifications for Recycled Content Products

Federal and state specifications for recycled content levels in various products have been established. The specifications address only those materials procured by federal or state agencies, respectively, and are implemented when economically and practically feasible. U.S. federal procurement guidelines are given in 40CFR Parts 247 through 253 and Illinois content requirements are given in Public Act 87-95. Recycled content levels for paper products, which have the largest effect on procurement, are shown in Table 7.1. As can be seen, Illinois has taken an aggressive stand in purchasing recycled content paper products for its state agencies.

Current State of Illinois specifications for procurement of recycled content xerographic paper are as follows (ILCMS, 1991):

- 20# basis weight white recycled xerographic bond paper to meet all requirements and specifications of a super premium No. 4 xerographic bond except for the following:

- The paper shall contain at least 50% recovered paper material. Such recovered material shall consist of at least 20% deinked or post-consumer material.

- The paper shall have a minimum brightness of 80.

Table 7.1 Recommended Minimum Recycled Content Standards for Paper and Paper Products, % by weight

Paper Product Type	Federal		State of Illinois	
	Waste Paper [a]	Post-Consumer	Waste Paper [a]	Post-Consumer [b]
Fine Paper [c]	50	-	50	20-50 [d]
Newsprint	-	40	-	40-80
Tissue and Toweling				
Toilet Tissue	-	20	-	25-45
Paper Towels	-	40	-	25-45
Paper Napkins	-	30	-	25-45
Facial Tissue	-	5	-	25-45
Doilies	-	40	-	25-45
Boxes				
Corrugated Boxes	-	35	-	35-55
Fiber Boxes	-	35	-	35-55
Brown papers (e.g., bags)	-	5	-	35-55
Paperboard				
Paperboard products	-	80	-	80-95
Pad Backing	-	90	-	80-95
Source	40CFR250		PA87-95	

a. 'Waste Paper' content includes 'Post-Consumer' content requirements. Waste paper refers to paper waste which is created following completion of the papermaking process. Examples included post-consumer paper, envelope cuttings, bindery trimmings, printing waste, obsolete inventories and unused stock.

b. Range shown is amount required by 7/1/94 (low end) and that required after 7/1/2000 (high end).

c. 'Fine Paper' generally refers to high grade bleached printing and writing papers and includes the following specific paper types. offset printing, xerographic, mimeo and duplicator, writing, stationary, office paper (e.g., note pads), paper for high speed copiers, envelopes, form bond (including computer and carbonless), book papers, bond papers, ledger, cover stock, and cotton fiber papers. Cotton fiber paper must contain 25% recovered cotton fiber or linen and 50% waste paper.

d. Either post-consumer materials or deinked stock. Phased in from 20% (min.) deinked stock or post-consumer materials by 7/1/94 to 50% (min.) after 7/1/2000.

7.4 Joint Purchasing

In order to obtain lower rates than may be achieved on their own and to simplify procurement, public community colleges and universities in Illinois may voluntarily purchase recycled content products through the state under a Joint Purchasing Agreement. It is necessary to be a 'governmental unit' in order to participate in the Joint Purchasing Program (a 'governmental unit' is any public authority which has the power to tax or any other public entity created by statute). Each governmental unit must obtain legal authority to participate in the Joint Purchasing Program from its governing board through the passage of a resolution. The joint purchasing agreement allows colleges (and cities and counties also) to piggyback on the State of Illinois Central Management Services (CMS) contract and the unit prices established under it. Following approval by the college board and approval by CMS, a college would directly contact contracted vendors, issue purchase orders, and arrange for delivery at the price set with the state's larger volume purchases without further involvement of CMS. Further assistance regarding the joint purchasing program through CMS can be obtained from the State of Illinois Joint Purchasing Manual at: T. Wurth, Joint Purchasing Program, Procurement Services Division, 801 Stratton Building, Springfield, IL, 62706, (217) 785-3900.

7.5 Sources of Recycled Content Products

The following publication summarize sources of recycled content products that are available for procurement:

> Recycled Products Guide
> PO Box 577
> Ogdensburg, NY 13669
> (800) 267-0707

It also publishes a monthly newsletter, "Recycled Products Guide Reporter," available from the same address. A number of waste and paper related publications regularly contain information regarding recycling and recycled content products (i.e., Recycled Paper News, Pulp & Paper Magazine, Fibre Market News, Resource Recycling, Recycling Today, Biocycle, Waste Age). Additional sources of information are given in the reference lists at the end of this report.

Appendix A   State of Illinois College Recycling Law

(Illinois Revised Statutes Ch. 111 1/2, new par. 7053.1)[a]

Sec. 3.1 Institutions of higher learning. (a) For purposes of this Section, "State-supported institutions of higher learning" or "institutions" means the University of Illinois, Southern Illinois University, the colleges and universities under the jurisdiction of the Board of Governors of State Colleges and Universities, the colleges and universities under the jurisdiction of the Board of Regents of Regency Universities, and the public community colleges subject to the Public Community College Act.

(b)   Each State-supported institution of higher learning shall develop a comprehensive waste reduction plan covering a period of 10 years which addresses the management of solid waste generated by academic, administrative, student housing and other institutional functions. The waste reduction plan shall be developed by January 1, 1995. The initial plan required under this Section shall be updated by the institution every 5 years, and any proposed amendments to the plan shall be submitted for review in accordance with subsection (f).

(c)   Each waste reduction plan shall address, at a minimum, the following topics: existing waste generation by volume, waste composition, existing waste reduction and recycling activities, waste collection and disposal costs, future waste management methods, and specific goals to reduce the amount of waste generated that is subject to landfill disposal.

(d)   Each waste reduction plan shall provide for recycling of marketable materials currently present in the institution's waste stream, including but not limited to landscape waste, corrugated cardboard, computer paper, and white office paper, and shall provide for the investigation of potential markets for other recyclable materials present in the institution's waste stream. The recycling provisions of the waste reduction plan shall

---

a. Excerpted from Public Act 86-1363

Appendix A   State of Illinois College Recycling Law

be designed to achieve, by January 1, 2000, at least a 40% reduction (referenced to a base year of 1987) in the amount of solid waste that is generated by the institution and identified in the waste reduction plan as being subject to landfill disposal.

(e)   Each waste reduction plan shall evaluate the institution's procurement policies and practices to eliminate procedures which discriminate against items with recycled content, and to identify products or items which are procured by the institution on a frequent or repetitive basis for which products with recycled content may be substituted. Each waste reduction plan shall prescribe that it will be the policy of the institution to purchase products with recycled content whenever such products have met specifications and standards of equivalent products which do not contain recycled content.

(f)   Each waste reduction plan developed in accordance with this Section shall be submitted to the Department of Energy and Natural Resources for review and approval. The Department's review shall be conducted in cooperation with the Board of Higher Education and the Illinois Community College Board.

(g)   The Department of Energy and Natural Resources shall provide technical assistance, technical materials, workshops and other information necessary to assist in the development and implementation of the waste reduction plans. The Department shall develop guidelines and funding criteria for providing grant assistance to institutions for the implementation of approved waste reduction plans.

Appendix B
Procedure for Determination of Waste Generation from Limited Sample Sizes

1. Scope

1.1 This method describes a procedure for estimating the quantities of waste collected by weighing a small but representative sample of refuse loads. The procedure applies to the determination of waste quantities in differing seasons of the year and applies to using collection devices of differing types (e.g., open top roll-off, rear load packer). It also applies to estimating waste quantities from differing establishments (e.g., housing, academic).

1.2 This procedure does not apply to waste disposal practices which continuously record vehicle load weights as a matter of policy.

1.3 This procedure does not determine the size of a sample for the purposes of determining composition.

1.4 Reference: Rushbrook, P., and Ball, R. 1988. "Improved Estimation of Waste Arisings Using Limited Sample Sizes" Waste Management & Research 6(1):35-44.

2. Definitions

2.1 Variables

	CI	Confidence interval
	E	maximum allowable error (e.g., $\pm 4\%$) based on a certain level of certainty (e.g., 95%)
	n	number of sample weighings
	N	Total number of refuse loads of a refuse container type (e.g., rear packer) in a season (e.g., winter)
	P	Percent of refuse vehicle loads to be weighed (i.e., $n = PN$)
	x	weight of refuse in a vehicle
	$\bar{x}$	mean weight of refuse for (n) sample weighings
	X	combined total weight for a type of refuse container (e.g., rear packer) in a season (e.g., winter)
	s	standard deviation of sample weighings
	S	standard deviation of loads
	t*	student's 't' value

Appendix B

2.2 Subscripts

a 1 - CI (e.g., for 95% level of confidence, a = 1-0.95 = 0.05)

i Season of the year (i.e., 1=winter, 2=spring, 3=summer, 4=fall)

j Refuse vehicle type (e.g., rear packer, roll off, yard box, lugger box, dumpster)

3. Summary of Method

3.1 The total number of samples to be weighed is based on the level of statistical confidence desired and the maximum allowable error.

3.2 One sample corresponds to one container or one vehicle load (the smallest unit of measurement).

3.3 Vehicles or containers are randomly chosen for sampling and weighed prior to being discharged.

3.4 The estimated annual (or periodic) tonnages are calculated from the limited number of samples weighed.

4. Significance and Use

4.1 Waste generation data is used in planning solid waste disposal needs, designing waste management facilities, and in measuring the impact of recycling and waste reduction.

4.2 Care should be taken to examine the seasonal variation of waste generation at universities and community colleges.

5. Apparatus

5.1 For weighing trucks, a truck scale with a capacity of at least 20,000 lbs and an accuracy of at least 100 lbs. should be used.

5.2 For weighing waste generation in smaller containers, a weigh scale with a capacity of at least 200 lb. and an accuracy of at least 1 lb. should be used.

6. Precautions

6.1 Review the precautions and procedures with the operating and sorting personnel prior to the conduct of the field activities.

Appendix B

7. Calibration

7.1 All weigh scale equipment shall be calibrated according to the manufacturer's instructions. Take appropriate corrective action if the readings are different than the calibration weights.

8. Procedures

8.1 Identify the types of refuse collection containers in use.

8.2 Determine the tare (empty) weight of all refuse container types.

8.3 Determination of appropriate sample size

8.3.1 When considering a waste disposal operation where no weighings have previously been recorded, it is impossible to determine in advance the appropriate sample sizes to take. The requisite sample size will be affected both by the level of accuracy required in the estimate and in the variation of refuse weights handled. If there is a small variation in vehicle refuse weights, then an accurate estimate can be obtained from a relatively small sample. On the other hand, if there is a wide variation in refuse weights, a larger sample is required for the same level of accuracy.

8.3.2 Assuming operations remain unchanged, it should only be necessary to go through the process of determining the most appropriate sample size the first year. A similar sample size should suffice in subsequent years.

8.3.3 There are two causes of error that affect the accuracy of a refuse weight estimate: (i) taking the sample means, $\overline{x_{ij}}$, as estimates of the actual population means; and (ii) assuming the sample mean has a normal distribution with the actual mean and standard deviation when the t distribution is correct. However, providing sample sizes are always greater than 30, the errors due to item ii can generally be ignored.

9. Calculations

9.1 Because the process is iterative, it is initially necessary to estimate the number of sample weighings (n) to be taken. A typical acceptable start is to weigh 5% of the total number of loads generated.

9.2 Calculation of annual tonnages

9.2.1 For individual refuse vehicle weighings, x, in a season (i) of collection vehicle type (j), the mean vehicle refuse weight, $\overline{x_{ij}}$, and standard deviation, s_{ij}, of n sample weighings (e.g., 5% of the total) is:

$$\overline{x_{ij}} = \frac{1}{n} \sum x_{ij}$$

Appendix B

$$S_{ij} = \sqrt{\frac{\sum(x_{ij} - \overline{x_{ij}})^2}{n_{ij} - 1}}$$

9.2.2 If there are N_{ij} total loads for a vehicle type in a season, then the mean seasonal tonnage (X_{ij}) is

$$X_{ij} = N_{ij} \cdot \overline{x_{ij}}$$

and the standard deviation for the total loads is

$$S_{ij} = \frac{N_{ij} \cdot s_{ij}}{\sqrt{n_{ij}}}$$

9.2.3 The corresponding annual tonnage (X_{Tj}) for a collection vehicle type j may then be determined by adding the four seasons of the year

$$X_{Tj} = X_{\text{total, vehicle type j}} = X_{1j} + X_{2j} + X_{3j} + X_{4j}$$

The annual tonnage standard deviation, S_j, and confidence limits, CI_j, can then be calculated as

$$S_j = \sqrt{S_{1j}^2 + S_{2j}^2 + S_{3j}^2 + S_{4j}^2}$$

$$CI_j = \pm z_{a/2} S_j,$$

where $z_{a/2}$ is the student's t value, generally for n samples greater than 30, and a = 1 - confidence limit desired (e.g., for a 95% level of confidence, a/2=0.025).

Therefore, the confidence limits (e.g., 95%) for a waste quantity estimate will be

$$X_{Tj} \pm CI_j$$

9.3 Combining vehicle categories

9.3.1 The combined mean annual tonnage, X_{TOTAL}, is determined by summing all vehicle categories

$$X_{TOTAL} = \sum_{k=1}^{j} X_{Tk}$$

9.3.2 The combined confidence interval for all vehicle types is

$$CI_j = \pm z_{a/2} \sqrt{\sum_{k=1}^{j} S_k^2}$$

Appendix B

9.4 Determining the appropriate number of samples, n

9.4.1 Determine the maximum allowable error, E, which is acceptable for the tonnage estimate (e.g., ±4%).

9.4.2 Determine the acceptable level of confidence to be utilized (typically 90% or 95%).

9.4.3 Identify the total number of loads handled each season for each refuse container/vehicle type (N_{ij}).

9.4.3 Estimate the percent of sample weighings, P, to be taken (i.e., 5% as indicated in section 9.1).

9.4.4 The number of sample weighings, n, for season i and vehicle type j is

$$n = P \cdot N_{ij}$$

9.4.5 The maximum allowable error will be met provided

$$\left[\frac{t^* \cdot s_{ij} / \sqrt{n}}{x_{ij}} \right] \leq E$$

Generally for a large number of samples (n>30), $t^* = 1.96$ for a 95% level of confidence and $t^* = 1.65$ for a 90% level of confidence. If the maximum allowable error (E) is not met, it is then necessary to enlarge the sample size (say to 10% of the total number of loads instead of 5%) and repeat the above procedure.

Appendix B

10. Example of Estimating Generation

An example of applying the model and comparing estimated quantities to real life measured data can now be made. The example is from a waste handling authority which weighed all of its loads during two quarters of the year. A sample size of 6% of the total loads for each quarter was chosen. An estimation of the mean and 95% confidence limits of all waste generated for the two quarters was desired. Also, the waste handling authority wanted to be 90% sure that the overall estimate using this method was was within $\pm 10\%$ of the true value.

10.1 Data and Assumptions:

1. 611 total loads per quarter for vehicle type A ($N_{1A} = N_{2A} = 611$)

2. 6% of the loads from vehicle type "A" are to be weighed during two quarters of the year.

3. The sample size is then $n_{1A} = n_{2A} = 611 \cdot 0.06 = 36.66 \approx 38$ (rounded up 1 in case of total number loads handled changes).

4. Vehicle tonnage data from 38 randomly chosen loads is shown in Tables B.1 and B.2

5. $E = \pm 10\%$

10.2 Calculations

1. First quarter (Table B.1) mean vehicle payload $\overline{x_{1A}}$ = 5.16 tons; standard deviation s_{1A} = 1.66 tons.

2. Second quarter (Table B.2) mean vehicle payload $\overline{x_{2A}}$ = 5.18 tons; standard deviation s_{2A} = 1.72 tons.

3. Estimated tonnage from vehicle type A for the first quarter is X_{1A} = $5.16 \cdot 611 = 3153$ tons.

   Since n > 30, it is possible to approximate the t distribution using the normal distribution. The seasonal tonnage standard deviation is then

   $$S_{1A} = \frac{611 \cdot 1.66}{\sqrt{38}} = 164.5 \text{ tons}$$

   The tonnage from vehicle type A for the second quarter is $X_{2A} = 5.18 \cdot 611 = 3165$ tons, with a season standard deviation of

   $$S_{1A} = \frac{611 \cdot 1.72}{\sqrt{38}} = 170.5 \text{ tons}$$

Appendix B

4. The tonnage for the six month period, or two seasons, is then $X_{TA} = X_{1A} + X_{2A} = 3153 + 3165 = 6318$ tons, with a standard deviation of

$$S_A = \sqrt{164.5^2 + 170.5^2} = 237 \text{ tons}$$

5. At the 95% confidence interval, $z_{a/2} = 1.96$ and therefore the six month tonnage will be

$$= 6318 \pm 1.96 \cdot 237$$
$$= 6318 \pm 465 \text{ tons}$$
i.e., 5853 to 6783 tons

10.3 Verification of appropriate sample size

1. For the first quarter:
$$\overline{x_{1A}} = 5.16 \text{ tons,}$$
$$s_{1A} = 1.66 \text{ tons,}$$
$$n_{1A} = 38$$

2. For a 90% level of confidence and n = 38, $t^* \approx t_\infty = 1.65$ (Table B.4)

3. The accuracy criterion of $\pm 10\%$ for the first quarter is met provided

$$\left[\frac{1.65 \cdot 1.66 / \sqrt{38}}{5.16}\right] \cdot 100\% = 8.6\% \leq 10\%$$

4. Therefore, the sample size for the first quarter is sufficient.

5. For the second quarter:
$$\overline{x_{2A}} = 5.18 \text{ tons,}$$
$$s_{2A} = 1.72 \text{ tons,}$$
$$n_{2A} = 38$$

6. The accuracy criterion of $\pm 10\%$ for the second quarter is met provided

$$\left[\frac{1.65 \cdot 1.72 / \sqrt{38}}{5.18}\right] \cdot 100\% = 8.9\% \leq 10\%$$

7. Therefore, the sample size for the second quarter is sufficient.

Appendix B

10.4 Comparison of Results with Actual Total

    1. Shown below are estimated and actual seasonal refuse weight data. The waste disposal authority which conducted the sampling also measured every refuse vehicle weight, which allows for comparison of estimated and actual values. It shows that a sampling of 6% of the vehicles yielded results well within the 95% confidence limits of $\pm$ 465 tons.

	Estimate (tons)	Actual (tons)	Difference (tons)	Difference (%)
1st quarter	3153	3102	+51	2.6
2nd quarter	3165	3238	-73	2.3
Total	6318	6340	-22	0.3

Appendix B

Table B.1   Quarter 1 Vehicle Tonnages from a Waste Collection Authority (tons)

Sampling Week Day of Week	1 Thursday	2 Tuesday	3 Friday	4 Monday
Quarter 1	3.19	4.80	5.37	7.74
	6.01	7.58	7.69	5.38
	6.94	5.36	4.00	5.15
	7.71	2.74	6.06	7.62
	3.30	3.08	2.45	6.91
	4.48	6.07	5.85	4.34
	6.78	4.02	4.86	5.62
	7.30	3.81		6.20
	5.05			3.19
	5.41			4.46
	1.82			
	2.71			
	4.89			
Number of Loads	13	8	7	10
Mean Vehicle Payload	= 5.16 (n=38)			
Standard Deviation	= 1.66			

Table B.2   Quarter 2 Vehicle Tonnages from a Waste Collection Authority (tons)

Sampling Week Day of Week	1 Wednesday	2 Thursday	3 Tuesday	4 Friday
Quarter 2	6.00	7.66	2.84	5.41
	6.58	7.22	7.23	4.93
	7.64	3.86	4.00	6.63
	6.95	8.23	5.11	3.23
	7.39	6.88	5.56	3.77
	5.96	7.51	5.54	4.73
	5.15	7.12	3.42	2.77
	3.04	4.05	3.85	
	2.96	4.27	1.69	
	4.31	4.32		
	5.44	3.42		
Number of Loads	11	11	9	7
Mean Vehicle Payload	= 5.18 (n=38)			
Standard Deviation	= 1.72			

Appendix C
Procedure for Determination of Waste Characterization

1. Scope

1.1　The method describes the procedures for measuring the composition of unprocessed municipal solid waste (MSW) by employing manual sorting. The procedure applies to the determination of the mean composition of MSW based on the collection and manual sorting of a number of samples of waste over a selected period of time with a minimum of one week.

1.2　The procedures include those for collection of a representative sorting sample of unprocessed waste, manual sorting of the waste into individual waste components, data reduction, and reporting of results.

1.3　Reference: ASTM D34.01.02 (Draft) Method for Determining the Composition of Unprocessed Municipal Solid Waste

2. Definitions

2.1　Variables

	e	maximum allowable error
	mf	mass fraction of a component
	n	number of samples required to achieve a desired level of error
	P	percentage of a waste stream component
	s	estimated standard deviation of a waste stream component
	$\bar{x}$	estimated mean value of a waste stream component
	t*	student's t statistic corresponding to the desired level of confidence
	w	weight of a component

2.2　Subscripts

	i	waste stream component (e.g., newspaper, white office paper)
	j	total number of waste stream components

2.3　<u>Sorting Sample</u>: A 200 to 300 lb portion that is deemed to represent the characteristics of a vehicle load of MSW.

Appendix C

2.4 <u>Composite Item</u>: An object in the waste that is composed of multiple waste components or dissimilar materials, such as disposable diaper, bi-metal beverage containers, electrical conductor composed of metallic wire encased in plastic insulation, etc.

3. Summary of Method

3.1 The number of samples to be sorted is calculated based upon statistical criteria selected by the investigators.

3.2 Vehicle loads of waste are designated for sampling, and a sorting sample is collected from the discharged vehicle load.

3.3 The sorting sample is manually sorted into waste components. The weight fraction of each component in the sorting sample is calculated from the weights of the components.

3.4 The mean waste composition is calculated using the results of the composition of each of the sorting samples.

4. Significance and Use

4.1 Waste composition information has wide application and can be used for such activities as solid waste planning, designing waste management facilities, and establishing a reference waste composition for use as a baseline standard in facility contracts and in acceptance test plans.

4.2 The method can be used to define and report the composition of municipal solid waste through the selection and manual sorting of samples of waste. Care should be taken to consider the source and seasonal variation of waste, where applicable.

4.3 After performing a waste composition analysis, laboratory analyses may be performed on representative samples of waste components or mixtures of waste components for purposes related to the planning, management, design, testing, and operation of resource recovery facilities.

5. Apparatus

5.1 Sufficient metal, plastic, or fiber containers for storing and weighing each waste component, labeled accordingly. For components that will have a substantial moisture content (e.g., food waste), metal or plastic containers are recommended to avoid absorption of moisture by the container and, thus, the need for a substantial number of weighings to maintain an accurate tare weight for the container.

5.2 A mechanical or electronic weigh scale with a capacity of at least 200 lb, and a precision of at least 0.1 lb.

Appendix C

5.3 Heavy-duty tarps, shovels, rakes, push brooms, dust pans, hand brooms, magnets, sorting table, first aid kit, miscellaneous small tools, traffic cones, traffic vests, leather gloves, hardhats, safety glasses, and leather boots.

6. Precautions

6.1 Review the precautions and procedures with the operating and sorting personnel prior to the conduct of the field activities.

6.2 Sharp objects such as nails, razor blades, hypodermic needles, and pieces of glass are present in solid waste. Personnel should be instructed of this danger and to brush waste particles aside while sorting, as opposed to projecting their hands with force into the mixture. Personnel handling and sorting solid waste should wear appropriate protection. Appropriate protection includes heavy leather gloves, dust masks, hardhats, safety glasses, and safety boots.

6.3 During the process of unloading waste from collection vehicles and of handling waste with heavy equipment, projectiles may issue from the mass the waste. The projectiles can include flying glass particles from breaking glass containers and metal lids from plastic and metal containers that burst under pressure when run over by heavy equipment. The problem is particularly severe when the waste handling surface is of high compressive strength, e.g., concrete. Personnel should be made aware of the danger and wear eye and head protection if in the vicinity of the collection vehicle unloading point, or in the vicinity of heavy equipment, or both.

6.4 Select a location for discharge of designated loads, manual sorting activities, and weighing operation that is flat, level, and away from the normal waste handling and processing areas.

6.5 Weigh storage containers each day, or more frequently if necessary, in order to maintain an accounting of the tare weight.

6.6 Loss of mass from the sorting sample can occur through evaporation of water. Consequently, samples should be sorted as soon as possible after collection.

6.7 Containers of liquids or other potentially dangerous wastes shall be put aside and handled by the crew chief.

7. Calibration

7.1 All weigh scale equipment shall be calibrated according to the manufacturer's instructions. Take appropriate corrective action if the readings are different than the calibration weights.

Appendix C

8. Procedures

8.1 Secure a flat and level area for discharge of the vehicle load. The surface should be swept clean or covered with a clean, durable tarp prior to discharge of the load.

8.2 Position the scale on a clean, flat, and level surface and adjust the level of the scale if necessary. Check the accuracy and operation of the scale with a known (i.e., reference) weight.

8.3 Weigh all empty storage containers and record the tare weights.

8.4 Determine the number of sorting samples to be sorted. The determination is a function of the waste components to be sorted and the desired precision as applied to each component. Weights of 200 to 300 lb for sorting samples of unprocessed solid waste are recommended. The number of samples is determined using the calculational method described in section 9.1.

8.5 A comprehensive list of waste components for sorting is shown in Table C.1. A description of some of the waste component categories is given in Table C.2. Other waste components can be defined and sorted depending upon the purpose of the waste composition determination. The list in Table C.1 is comprised of those components most commonly used to define and report the composition of solid waste. At a minimum, it is recommended that the complement of left-justified categories in Table C.1 be sorted. Therefore, similar breakdowns of solid waste composition are available for purposes of comparison, if desired. Label the storage containers accordingly.

8.6 Vehicles for sampling shall be selected at random during each day of the one-week sampling period, or so as to be representative of the waste stream as agreed to by the affected parties. With respect to random selection of vehicles, any method is acceptable that does not introduce a bias into the selection. An acceptable method is use of a random number generator. For a weekly sampling period of k days, the number of vehicles sampled each day shall be approximately n/k, where n is the total number of vehicle loads to be selected for determination of waste composition. A weekly period is defined to be 5 to 7 days.

8.7 Direct the designated vehicle containing the load of waste to the area secured for discharge of the load and collection of the sorting sample.

8.8 Collect any required information from the vehicle operator prior to the vehicle leaving the discharge area. Direct the vehicle operator to discharge the load onto the clean surface in one contiguous pile, i.e., to avoid gaps in the discharged load in order to facilitate the collection of the samples.

8.9 Using a front-end loader with at least a one cubic yard bucket, remove material longitudinally along one entire side of the discharged load, sufficient to form a mass of material which, on a visual basis, is at least four times the desired weight of the sorting sample (i.e., about 1,000 lb). Mix, cone and quarter the material and select one quarter to be the sorting sample, using a random method of selection or a sequence agreed to by all affected parties, for the purpose of eliminating or minimizing biasing of the sample.

Appendix C

If an oversize item (e.g., water heater) composes a large weight percentage of the sorting sample, add a notation on the data sheet and weigh it, if possible. Unprocessed solid waste is a heterogeneous mixture of materials. Consequently, care must be taken during the application of the procedures for sample collection in order to obtain a representative-sample.

8.10 One sorting sample is selected from each collection vehicle load that is designated for sampling. All handling and manipulation of the discharged load, longitudinal sample, and sorting sample shall be conducted on previously cleaned surfaces. If necessary, remove the sorting sample to a secured manual sorting area. The sorting may be placed on a clean table for sorting for the convenience of the sorting personnel. The sorting area shall be a previously cleaned, flat, and level surface.

8.11 Position the storage containers around the sorting sample. From the sorting sample, empty all containers such as capped jars, paper bags, and plastic bags of their contents. Segregate each waste item and place it in the appropriate storage container.

8.12 In the case of composite items found in the waste, separate the individual materials where practical and place the individual materials into the appropriate storage containers. Where impractical, segregate and the crew chief shall classify the composite item according to the following order:

8.12.1 If there are many identical composite items (e.g., plastic-sheathed aluminum electrical conductor), place them into the waste component containers corresponding to the materials present in the item and in the approximate proportions according to the estimated mass fraction of each material in the item.

8.12.2 If there are only a few of the identical composite items, place them in the storage container corresponding to the material which comprises, on a weight basis, the majority of the item (e.g., place bi-metal beverage cans in the ferrous container).

8.12.3 If composite items represent substantial weight percentages of the sorting sample, a separate category should be established (e.g., composite roofing shingles).

8.12.4 If none of the above procedures is appropriate, place the item(s) in the storage container labeled "Other Non-Combustible" or "Other Combustible" as appropriate.

8.13 Sorting continues until the maximum particle size of the remaining waste particles is approximately 0.5 in. At this point, apportion the remaining particles into the storage containers corresponding to the waste components represented in the remaining mixture. The apportionment shall be accomplished by making a visual estimate of the mass fraction of waste components represented in the remaining mixture.

8.14 Record the gross weights of the storage containers and of any waste items sorted but not stored in containers. The data sheet shown as Form 3 (Appendix D) can be used to record gross weights as well as tare weights.

Appendix C

8.15 After recording the gross weights, empty the storage containers and weigh them again, if appropriate. Re-weighting is important and necessary if the containers become moisture-laden, e.g., from wet waste.

8.16 Clean the sorting site as well as the load discharge area of all waste materials.

9. Calculations

9.1 Number of 200 to 300 lb samples.

9.1.1 The number of sorting samples (i.e., vehicle loads) (n) required to achieve a desired level of measurement precision is a function of the component(s) under consideration and the confidence level. The governing equation for n is:

$$n = \left[\frac{t^* \cdot s}{e \cdot x}\right]^2 \qquad (1)$$

where t^* is the student t statistic corresponding to the desired level of confidence, s is the estimated standard deviation, e is the desired level of precision, and x is the estimated mean.

All numerical values for the symbols are in decimal notation. For example, a value of precision (e) of 20% is represented as 0.2.

One sorting sample is chosen per vehicle load.

Suggested values of s and of x for waste components are listed in Tables C.3 and C.4 for college waste and standard municipal waste, respectively. Values of t^* are given in Table C.5 for 90% and 95% levels of confidence, respectively.

9.1.2 Estimate the number of samples (n') for the selected conditions (i.e., precision and level of confidence) and components using equation 1. For the purpose of estimation, select from Table C.5 the t^* value for $n = \infty$ for the the selected level of confidence. Since the required number of samples will vary among the components for a given set of conditions, a compromise will be required in terms of selecting a sample size, i.e., the number of samples that will be sorted. The component that is chosen to govern the precision of the composition measurement (and therefore the number of samples required for sorting) is termed the "governing component" for the purpose of this method.

9.1.3 After determining the governing component and its corresponding number of samples (n_o), return to Table C.5 and select the student t statistic (t_o^*) corresponding to n_o. Recalculate the number of samples, i.e., n', using (t_o^*).

Appendix C

    9.1.4 Compare n_o to the new estimate of n, i.e., n', which was calculated for the governing component. If the values differ by more than 10%, repeat the calculations of 9.1.2 and 9.1.3.

    9.1.5 If the values are within 10%, select the larger value as the number of samples to be sorted. Refer to section 10 for a sample calculation of n.

9.2 Component Composition

    9.2.1 The component composition of solid waste is reported on the basis of the mass fraction (expressed as a decimal) or percentage of waste component t in the solid waste mixture. The reporting is on the basis of wet weight, i.e., the weight of materials immediately after sorting.

    9.2.2 The mass fraction of component i, mf_i, is defined and computed as:

$$mf_i = \frac{w_i}{\sum_{i=1}^{j} w_i} \quad (2)$$

where w_i is the weight of component i and j is the number of waste components. In those cases where a container is used to store and weigh the materials:

$$w_i = \text{gross weight - tare weight of container} \quad (3)$$

    9.2.3 The percentage of component i, P_i, is defined and computed as:

$$P_i = mf_i \cdot 100 \quad (4)$$

    9.2.4 For the data analysis to be correct, the denominator of equation (2) must be unity and,

$$\sum_{i=1}^{j} P_i = 100 \quad (5)$$

9.3 The mean component composition for the one-week period is calculated using the component composition results from each of the analysis samples: The mean mass fraction of component i, $\overline{mf_i}$, is calculated as:

$$\overline{mf_i} = \frac{1}{n} \sum_{k=1}^{n} (mf_i)_k \quad (6)$$

Appendix C

and the mean percentage of component i, $\overline{P_i}$, is calculated as,

$$\overline{P_i} = \frac{1}{n} \sum_{k=1}^{n} (P_i)_k \qquad (7)$$

where n is the number of samples.

10. Example of Estimating the Number of Samples (n) Required for Analysis

Assumptions:

1. Corrugated is selected as the governing component
2. A 90% confidence level is selected
3. A precision of 10% is desired

Therefore:

s = 0.06 (from Table C.4)
x = 0.14 (from Table C.4)
e = 0.10
t* (n=∞) = 1.645 (from Table C.5)

Using equation 1:

$$n = \left[\frac{t^* \cdot s}{e \cdot x}\right]^2$$

$$n = \left[\frac{1.645 \cdot 0.06}{0.1 \cdot 0.14}\right]^2$$

$$= 50$$

$$= n_o$$

Referring again to Table C.5, for n = 50

$$t^*_{90} (n = 50) = 1.677$$

and,

$$n = \left[\frac{1.677 \cdot 0.06}{0.1 \cdot 0.14}\right]^2$$

$$= 52$$

$$= n'$$

Since 52 (i.e., n') is within 10% of 50 (i.e., n_o), 52 samples should be selected for analysis.

Appendix C

Table C.1 Typical Waste Component Categories

Mixed Paper	Other Organics
High Grade Paper	Ferrous
Computer Printout	Cans
Other Office Paper	Other Ferrous
Newsprint	Aluminum
Corrugated	Cans
Plastic	Foil
PET Bottles	Other Aluminum
HDPE Bottles	Glass
Film	Clear
Other Plastic	Brown
Yard Waste	Green
Food Waste	Other Inorganics
Wood	Landscape Waste

Appendix C

Table C.2 Description of Some Waste Component Categories

Category	Description
Mixed Paper	Office paper, computer paper, magazines, glossy paper, waxed paper, other paper not fitting categories of "Newsprint" and "Corrugated"
Newsprint	Newspaper
Corrugated	Corrugated medium, corrugated boxes or cartons, brown (kraft) paper (i.e., corrugated) bags
Plastic	All plastics
Landscape Waste	Branches, twigs, leaves, grass, other plant material
Food Waste	All food waste except bones
Wood	Lumber, wood products, pallets, furniture
Other Organics/ Combustibles	Textiles, rubber, leather, other primarily burnable materials not included in the above component categories
Ferrous	Iron, steel, tin cans, bi-metal cans
Aluminum	Aluminum, aluminum cans, aluminum foil
Glass	All glass
Other Inorganics/ Non-combustibles	Rock, sand, dirt, ceramics, plaster, non-ferrous non-aluminum metals (copper, brass, etc.), bones

Appendix C

Table C.3 Values of Mean and of Standard Deviation (s) for Within Week Sampling to Determine College Waste Component Composition [a]

Component	Standard Deviation	Mean
High Grade Office	0.08	0.15
Newsprint	0.05	0.11
Corrugated	0.03	0.10
Other Paper	-	0.30
Plastic	0.03	0.07
Yard Waste	-excluded-	
Food Waste	0.06	0.09
Wood	0.01	0.03
Ferrous	0.03	0.02
Aluminum	0.01	0.02
Glass	0.03	0.06
Other	-	<u>0.05</u>
		1.00

a. The tabulated mean values and standard deviations are estimates based on the averages shown in Chapter 3.

Table C.4 Values of Mean and of Standard Deviation (s) for Within Week Sampling to Determine MSW Component Composition [a]

Component	Standard Deviation	Mean
Mixed Paper	0.05	0.22
Newsprint	0.07	0.10
Corrugated	0.06	0.14
Plastic	0.03	0.09
Yard Waste	0.14	0.04
Food Waste	0.03	0.10
Wood	0.06	0.06
Other Organics	0.06	0.05
Ferrous	0.03	0.05
Aluminum	0.004	0.01
Glass	0.05	0.08
Other Inorganics	0.03	<u>0.06</u>
		1.00

a. The tabulated mean values and standard deviations are estimates based on field test data reported for municipal solid waste sampled during weekly sampling periods at several locations around the U.S.

Appendix C

Table C.5 Values of t Statistics (t*) as a Function of Number of Samples and Conference Interval

No. of Samples (n)	90%	95%
2	6.314	12.706
3	2.920	4.303
4	2.353	3.182
5	2.132	2.776
6	2.015	2.571
7	1.943	2.447
8	1.895	2.365
9	1.860	2.306
10	1.833	2.262
11	1.812	2.228
12	1.796	2.201
13	1.782	2.179
14	1.771	2.160
15	1.761	2.145
16	1.753	2.131
17	1.746	2.120
18	1.740	2.110
19	1.734	2.101
20	1.729	2.093
21	1.725	2.086
22	1.721	2.080
23	1.717	2.074
24	1.714	2.069
25	1.711	2.064
26	1.708	2.060
27	1.706	2.056
28	1.703	2.052
29	1.701	2.048
30	1.699	2.045
31	1.697	2.042
36	1.690	2.030
41	1.684	2.021
46	1.679	2.014
51	1.676	2.009
61	1.671	2.000
71	1.667	1.994
81	1.664	1.990
91	1.662	1.987
101	1.660	1.984
121	1.658	1.980
141	1.656	1.977
161	1.654	1.975
189	1.653	1.973
201	1.653	1.972
∞	1.645	1.960

Appendix D
Form 1   Building Waste Assessment Form

Date / /
Page of

Name of Building: _____

Address: _____

Building Functions (%)
- _____ Administrative / Office
- _____ Classroom
- _____ Computer Facilities
- _____ Food Service
- _____ Recreational
- _____ Residence
- _____ Vending
- _____ Health Services

Building Recycling Coordinator _____
Position   _____
Phone Number   _____

Description of Waste Disposal Paths in Building

Observed Composition (by volume) of Refuse in Building Dumpsters:

Building Personnel Comments

Janitorial Staff Comments

Appendix D
Form 2 Waste Disposal Inventory Assessment Form

Date / /
Page of

A	B	C	D	E	F	G	H
Location	Name of Hauler (or self-hauled)	Type and Size of Containers (cubic yards)	Number of Containers	Number of Pulls per Week	% Full when Emptied	Total Volume of Waste per Week (cubic yards) $(C \times D \times E \times F)$	Ownership of Refuse Container
			Total			Total	

Appendix D
Form 3 Waste Composition Data Sheet

Date / /
Page   of

Component	A Gross Weight (lbs)	B Tare Weight (lbs)	C Net Weight (lbs) (A - B)	D Density (lbs/ft³)	E Volume (ft³) (C/D)	F Volume % (E/E11)	G Weight % (C/C11)
1. Aluminum							
Cans							
Foil							
Other Aluminum							
2. Ferrous							
Cans							
Other ferrous							
3. Food Waste							
4. Glass							
Clear							
Brown							
Green							
5. Landscape Waste							
6. Paper							
Corrugated							
High Grade Paper							
Computer Printout							
White Ledger							
Mixed Paper							
Newspaper							
7. Plastic							
PET Bottles							
HDPE Bottles							
Film							
Other Plastic							
8. Wood							
9. Other Inorganics							
10. Other Organics							
11. Totals							

Appendix D
Form 4 Material Recycling Estimation Form

Date / /
Page   of

Material	A % by Weight in MSW (Form 3)	B Annual MSW Generation (Procedure B)	C Component Generation in MSW (A x B)	D Source Separated Amount (eg, recycled, composted	E Total Component Generation (C + D)	F Target Capture Efficiency (%)	G Target Recovery Amounts (E x F)
Totals							Total Targeted for Recycling

Appendix E   Weight / Volume Conversions for Recyclables and Waste Stream Components

Table E.1   Waste and True Material Densities

Material	Densitiy (lb/yd^3)
Municipal Waste:	100-200
After dumping from compactor truck	350-400
In compactor truck	500-700
In landfill	500-900
Shredded Waste	600-900
Baled in paper baler	800-1200
Bulk Densities:	
Cardboard	1.87
Aluminum	2.36
Plastics	2.37
Miscellaneous paper	3.81
Garden waste	4.45
Newspaper	6.19
Rubber	14.90
Glass	18.45
Food	23.04
True Densities:	
Wood	37
Cardboard	43
Paper	44-72
Glass	156
Aluminum	168
Steel	480
Polypropylene	56
Polyethylene	59
Polystyrene	65
ABS	64
Acrylic	74
Polyvinylchloride (PVC)	78

Table E.2   Recyclable Materials

Material	Volume	Weight (lbs)	Weight (tons)
Aluminum cans	1 full grocery bag	1.5	0.00075
Aluminum cans	55 gallon plastic bag	13-20	0.0065-0.01
Aluminum cans, flattened	1 cubic yard	250	0.125
Aluminum cans, whole	1 cubic yard	50-74	0.025-0.037
Corrugated Cardboard, loose	1 cubic yard	300	0.15
Corruagted Cardboard, baled	1 cubic yard	1,000-1,200	0.5-0.6
Ferrous cans, whole	1 cubic yard	150	0.075
Ferrous cans, flattened	1 cubic yard	850	0.425
Glass, whole bottles	1 cubic yard	600-1,000	0.3-0.5
Glass, semicrushed	1 cubic yard	1,000-1,800	0.5-0.9
Glass, crushed mechanically	1 cubic yard	800-2,700	0.4-1.35
Glass, whole bottles	1 full grocery bag	16	0.008
Glass, uncrushed-manually broken	55 gallon drum	125-500	0.0652-0.25
Grass clippings	1 cubic yard	400	0.2
Leaves, compacted	1 cubic yard	450	0.225
Leaves, uncompacted	1 cubic yard	250	0.125
Leaves, vacuumed	1 cubic yard	350	0.175
Newsprint	12" stack	35	0.0175
Newsprint, loose	1 cubic yard	360-800	0.18-0.4
Newsprint, compacted	1 cubic yard	720-1,000	0.36-0.5
PET bottles, whole, loose	1 cubic yard	30-40	0.15-0.02
PET bottles, whole, loose	1 gaylord [a]	40-53	0.02-0.0265
PET bottles, baled	30" by 48" by 62" bale	500	0.25
PET bottles, granulated	1 gaylord	700-750	0.35-0.375
PET bottles, granulated	tractor trailer load	30,000	15.0
Film, baled	30" by 42" by 48" bale	1,100	0.55
Film, baled	trailor load	44,000	22.0
HDPE dairy, whole, loose	1 cubic yard	24	0.012
HDPE dairy, baled	30" by 48" by 60" bale	500-800	0.25-0.4
HDPE mixed, baled	30" by 48" by 60" bale	600-900	0.3-0.45
HDPE mixed, granulated	gaylord	800-1,000	0.4-0.4
HDPE mixed, granulated	tractor trailer load	42,000	21
Mixed PET & dairy, whole, loose	cubic yard	average 32	0.016
Mixed PET, dairy & rigid, whole, loose	1 cubic yard	average 38	0.019
Used motor oil	1 gallon	7	0.0035
Tire, passenger car	one	12	0.006
Tire, truck	one	60	0.03
Food waste, solid & liquid fats	55 gallon drum	412	0.206
Wood chips	1 cubic yard	500	0.25

a. Gaylord (container) size most commonly used: 40" by 48" by 36"

Appendix F

Table F.1 Recycling Activities and Waste Disposal/Recycling Contacts at Illinois Public Universities

University	Town	Phone	Waste Disposal Contact	Title	Recycling Activities
Chicago State University	95th and King Drive Chicago, IL 60628	312-995-2140 312-995-2042 312-995-2140 312-995-2140	Gwendolyn Allen* Kristie Rogers* Diane Johnson* John Aycox#	Eng. & Planning Spec. Asst. to VP Admin Affairs Proj. Mgr. ENR Grants Bldg. Svcs. Supervisor	reuse boxes, mulch yardwaste
Eastern Illinois University	Charleston, IL 61920	217-581-2178	Gary Hanebrink Bob Propst	Supt. Building Maintenance Building Services Supv.	paper
Governor's State University	University Park, IL 60466	708-534-5000 x 2175, x 2181	Dee Woods* Mike Foley#	Dir. Purchasing Dir. Physical Plant	white paper
Illinois State University	Normal, IL 61761	309-438-2032 309-438-5966	Chuck Scott# Dave Deant#	Grounds Superintendant Office of Residential Life	
Northeastern Illinois University	5500 N. St. Louis Chicago, IL 60625	312-583-4050 x 2773 312-794-2878	James MacDonald* Michael Fulli*#	Chair. Recycling Cmte. Supt. Building Services	
Northern Illinois University	DeKalb, IL 60115	815-753-9545	Pat Hewitt* David Broustis*	Assoc. to V.P. Bus. & Ops.	
Sangamon State University	Springfield, IL 62794-9243	815-753-9793 217-786-6530	Ed Heiston# Richard R. Williams	Asst. Supt. Bldg Services Dir. Physical Plannning and Operations	paper, glass, cans
Southern Illinois University	Carbondale, IL 62901	618-453-8187 618-536-7511	Bruce Francis# John Meister*	Supt. Grounds Dir. Pollution Control	
Southern Illinois University	Edwardsville, IL 62026	618-692-3789	William Lyke*#	Asst. Dir. Physical Plant	paper
University of Illinois at Chicago	Chicago, IL 60680	312-996-2837	Robert Getz*#	Assoc. Dir Physical Plant	Al. cans, paper

Appendix F

Table F.1 (cont.)

University	Town	Phone	Waste Disposal Contact	Title	Recycling Activities
University of Illinois at Urbana	1501 South Oak St. Champaign, IL 61820	217-333-3070	Tim Hoss Vonne Ortiz Stan Kiser	Recycling Coordinator Recycling Coordinator, Housing Assoc. Dir. Facilities	
Western Illinois University	Macomb, IL 61455	309-295-1414	Phil Keefauver # Deborah Miller	Supv. Building Services University Relations	Al Cans

'*' Indicates a member of the college's recycling committee
'#' Indicates responsible for waste disposal

Appendix F

Table F.2 Recycling Activities and Waste Disposal/Recycling Contacts at Illinois Public Community Colleges

Community College	Town	Phone	Waste Disposal Contact	Title	Recycling Activities
Belleville Area College	2500 Carlyle Road Belleville, IL 62221	618-235-2700 x 285	David Buesch	Supt. Bldgs & Grounds	pilot paper program
Black Hawk College	6600 34th Ave Moline, IL 61265	309-796-1311 x 1369	Don Sproul	Dir. Facilities	Al cans, shred paper
City-Wide College	226 West Jackson Chicago, IL 60606-6997	312-641-2595 x 3014	Virginia McGann	Building Manager	
Daley College (Richard J.)	7500 S Pulaski Rd. Chicago, IL 60652	312-838-4859	Peter O'Connor	Chief Engineer	
Danville Area Community College	2000 East Main St. Danville, IL 61832-5199	217-443-8831	Richard Donahue	Dir. of Physical Plant	Al cans, computer paper
Du Page, College of	22nd & Lambert Rd. Glen Ellyn, IL 60137	708-858-2800 x 2017	Laura Galto	Mgr. of Staff Services	White & colored paper, Al cans
Elgin Community College	1700 Spartan Drive Elgin, IL 60120	708-697-1000	John Zeigler	Supv., Op. & Maint.	paper
Frontier Community College	Rural Route #1 Fairfield, IL 62837	618-842-3711	Galen Dunn	Maint. Dept.	
Harper College	Algonquin & Roselle Rds. Palatine, IL 60067	708-397-3000 x 2350	Charles Hearn	Custodial Supv.	Al. cans, paper

Appendix F

Table F.2 (cont.)

Community College	Town	Phone	Waste Disposal Contact	Title	Recycling Activities
Heartland Community College	1540 East College Suite 5 Nomal, IL 61761	309-452-4999	n.a.	n.a.	n.a.
Highland Community College	Pearl City Road Freeport, IL 61032	815-235-6121 x 300	Ed Stevens Barb Edler	Dir. Phys. Plant Facilities Coord.	paper
Illinois Central College	East Peoria, IL 61635	309-694-5121 309-694-5456	John Vogelsang Bob Wegner	Supv., Custodial Dept. Facilities Services	cancelled by haulers
Illinois Valley Community College	2578 E. 350th Rd. Oglesby, IL 61348	815-224-2720 x 300	Doug Renkosik	Dir. Phys. Plant	paper
Joliet Junior College	1216 Houbolt Ave. Joliet, IL 60436-9352	815-729-9020 x 396, x 241	Ken Pierce Dianne Schidt	Dir. Phys. Plant Dir. Admin. Svc.	Al. cans, computer paper
Kankakee Community College	Box 888 River Road Kankakee, IL 60901-0888	815-933-0230	John Haley	Dir. Phys. Plant	Al. cans, paper
Kaskaskia College	Shattuc Rd. Centralia, IL 62801-9285	618-532-1981 x 230	Dwayne Kessler	V.P. Finance & Ops.	
Kishwaukee College	Hwy 38 & Malta Malta, IL 60150	815-825-2086 x 270	Dianne McNeilly	Dean Liberal Arts Recycling Coordinator	mixed & white paper, Al. cans, glass, oil
Kennedy-King College	6800 S. Wentworth Chicago, IL 60621-3799	312-962-3724 x 721	Michael Collins	Engineer Maint. Dept.	

Appendix F

Table F.2 (cont.)

Community College	Town	Phone	Waste Disposal Contact	Title	Recycling Activities
Lake County, College of	19351 West Washington Grayslake, IL 60030	708-223-6601 x 248	Dean Yost	Dir. Physical Facilities	Al. cans, paper, phone books
Lake Land College	South Route #45 Mattoon, IL 61938	217-235-3131 x 284	Durward Askew	Dir. Maintenance	
Lewis & Clark Community College	5800 Godfrey Rd. Godfrey, IL 62035	618-466-3411 x 3100	Bob Breden	Dir. Auxilliary Svcs. & Facilities Operations	
Lincoln Land Community College	Shepherd Rd. Springfield, IL 62794-9256	217-786-2303	John Costello	Dir. Builings & Grounds	
Lincoln Trail College	Rural Route #3 Robinson, IL 62454	618-544-8657 x 1152	Jofn Kasinger	Supv. Building & Grounds Dept.	OCC
Logan College (John A.)	Route #2 Carterville, IL 62918	612-985-2828 x 332	Mike Jakubco	Supv. Grounds Mnt.	Al. cans
Malcom X College	1900 W. Van Buren Chicago, IL 60612-3197	312-942-3000 x 207	Charles Whitehead	Chief Engineer	
McHenry County College	Route #14-Lucas Rd. Crystal Lake, IL 60014	815-455-8564	Scott Selcke	Dir. Bldgs & Grnds	Al. cans

Appendix F

Table F.2 (cont.)

Community College	Town	Phone	Waste Disposal Contact	Title	Recycling Activities
Moraine Valley Community College	10900 S. 88th Ave. Palos Hills, IL 60465	708-974-5724	Ron Kurfirst	Dir. Campus Ops.	computer paper
Morton College	3801 S. Central Cicero, IL 60650	708-656-8000 x 220	Gary Stanley	Dir. Physical Plant	Al. cans, white office paper
Oakton Community College	1600 East Golf Rd. Des Plaines, IL 60016-1258	708-635-1780	Michael Biskin	Director Facilities	Al. cans
Olive-Harvey College	10001 S. Woodlawn Chicago, IL 60628	312-568-3700	John Kenny	Chief Engineer	
Olney Central College	305 North West St. Olney, IL 62450	618-395-4351 x 2300	Kirk Voght	Dir. Environmental Services	
Parkland College	2400 W. Bradley Champaign, IL 61821-1899	217-351-2211	Denny Elimon	Dir. Physical Plant & Purchasing	Al. cans, paper, glass
Prarie State College	202 S. Halsted St. Chicago Heights, IL 60411-1275	708-709-3701	Ray Marthaler	Dir. Physical Plant	
Rend Lake College	Rural Route #1 Ina, IL 62846-9740	618-437-5321 x 255, x 256	Pow Smith	Dir. Physical Plant	Al. cans
Richland Community College	1 College Park Decatur, IL 62521-8513	217-875-7200 x 549	David Holtsreter	Dir. Operations & Purchasing	Al. cans

Appendix F

Table F.2 (cont.)

Community College	Town	Phone	Waste Disposal Contact	Title	Recycling Activities
Rock Valley College	3301 N. Mulford Rockford, IL 61101	815-654-4269 815-654-4303	Richard Bernardi Harry Grady	Chmn. Maintenance Dir. Plant Operations	Al. cans, pilot paper
Sandburg College (Carl)	P.O. Box 1407 2232 South Lake Storey Rd. Galesburg, IL 61401	309-344-2518	Bob Adcock	Dir. Bldg. & Grounds	Al. cans
Sauk Valley Community College	173 Ill. Route #2 Dixon, IL 61201-9110	815-288-5511 x 299	Ross Herren	Dir. Bldgs & Grounds	paper
Shawnee Community College	Shawnee College Rd. Ullin, IL 62992	618-634-2242 x 210	Herman Lawrence	Supt. Bldgs & Grounds	paper, ONP, Al. cans, some PS
Southeastern Illinois College	Rural Route #4 College Drive Harrisburg, IL 62946-9477	618-252-6376 x 369			
South Suburban College of Cook Cty.	15800 S. State St. South Holland, IL 60473-1262	708-596-2000 x 484	Don Manning	Dir. Physical Plant Services	
Spoon River College	Rural Route #1 Canton, IL 61520-9801	309-647-4645 x 206, x 275	Dick Strode Ed Georgieff	Dir. Maintenance Head of Student Government	
State Community College	601 James R. Thompson Blvd. East St. Louis, IL 62201	618-583-2500	Cheryl Campbell	Dir. Business & Administration Dept.	

Appendix F

Table F.2 (cont.)

Community College	Town	Phone	Waste Disposal Contact	Title	Recycling Activities
Triton College	2000 Fifth Ave. River Grove, IL 60171	708-456-0300 x 204, x 410	Vito Bianco Dan Gallante		
Truman College (Harry S.)	1145 W. Wilson Chicago, IL 60640	312-989-3851	John Fallon	Chief Engineer	
Wabash Valley College	200 College Dr. Carmel, IL 62863	618-262-8641 x 3290	James Bogard	Supt. Buildings & Grounds	
Washington College (Harold)	30 East Lake St. Chicago, IL 60601	312-984-2868	Carl Shelley	Building Manager	
Waubonsee Community College	Illinois Route 47 at Harter Rd. P.O. Box 508 Sugar Grove, IL 60554	708-466-4811 x 212	Tom Carpus	Dir. Bldgs & Grounds	Al. cans, paper
Wood Community College (John)	150 South 48th St. Quincy, IL 62301	217-224-6500 x 112	Rob Hilgenbrink	Dean Business Services	paper
Wright College (Wilbur)	3400 N. Austin Chicago, IL 60634	312-794-3144 312-794-3262	Roger May Dan Fitzmaurice	Dean Student Activities Chief Engineer Maintenance	

Appendix G   Example Agreements for Marketing Recyclables

ABC PAPER COMPANY

January 31, 1991

Mr. Recycling Coordinator
Anytown Recycling Program
Anytown, MI 66208

Dear Mr. Coordinator:

The ABC Company in Papermill, Ohio is happy to provide you with this Letter of Intent regarding the recycled paper output from the City of Anytown, Michigan.

It is the intention of ABC Company, in mutual agreement with the City of Anytown, Michigan, to purchase old corrugated containers, brown grocery bags, old newspapers, and possibly office waste or direct mail, from the City of Anytown, provided it is available in clean, dry, and loose condition. We would prefer that the old corrugated and brown grocery bags be separated from the old newspapers and direct mail.

ABC Company guarantees to pay the Official Board Market (yellow sheet) price, average between high and low side, for the Detroit/Midwest area, less $30 per ton baling cost, with a guaranteed floor of zero ($0) dollars per ton. We would expect to receive approximately 9,000 tons per year of old corrugated and brown grocery bags, and approximately 7,000 tons per year of old newspapers and direct mail. We would pay this amount, provided the material was delivered to our plant at 4544 S. Walnut St. If we had to pick up the material at some central location, then the price would be adjusted based on the location and the method of pickup for the material.

We would like to negotiate a five-year contract for this material, with the option to renew the contract each year on the anniversary date, or some other satisfactory method of renewing the contract, a minimum of one year prior to the expiration date.

We are quite anxious to work with Anytown, as soon as possible, and to help them solve their solid waste problem.

Sincerely yours,

John R. Buyer
ABC Company

Exhibit G.1   Example Letter of Intent for Waste Paper Recycling (USEPA, 1991a)

Appendix G (cont.)

XYZ COMPANY
987 Johnson Road
Anytown, MI 12345

August 27, 1990

Mr. John Recycler
Universal Recycling Company
10 Main Street
Anytown, MI 12345

RE: Letter of Agreement for Office Paper Collection at XYZ Company

Dear Mr. Recycler:

Listed below are the terms of the agreement between XYZ Company and your firm for the removal of computer printout, white ledger office waste paper, and aluminum cans from the XYZ Building located at 987 Johnson Road, Anytown, MI.

1. Your firm will supply storage containers for the storage for two grades of paper and aluminum cans free of charge for use in the program to ensure compatibility with your truck and equipment. Your company will supply labor to deliver empty containers and remove full container from the dock storage area.

2. A regular collection schedule will be established during the first two months of service. However, if the containers reach premature capacity, we will call your firm for you to service our building as soon as possible to pick up the full hampers from the storage location and replace them with empty ones. Your driver will leave a signed receipt indicating amount of any and all pickups.

3. Computer printout and white ledger paper will be presented for sale to your firm based on your acceptable and non-acceptable conditions for contaminants.

4. Your removal of paper and aluminum shall constitute a sale to your firm. The purchase price for the paper will be based upon the grade listing in the Fibre Market News, a trade journal of the recycling industry and appropriate to the Anytown market area.

5. When old files from Records Retention have satisfied their retention period, we will phone your office to make special arrangements for your pick up and payment of these old records and files.

Exhibit G.2   Example Office Paper Collection Letter of Agreement (USEPA, 1991a)

Appendix G (cont.)

August 27, 1990
Page 2

6. Within 30 days after each calendar month you will forward to XYZ Company a check for the paper and aluminum sold to you during the preceding month with a statement describing your calculations.

7. Your firm will provide a monthly report which states the guaranteed price for the waste for that month, and showing year-to-date and monthly totals by waste grade.

8. It is understood that if after three pick ups the minimum weight per container is inaccurate, you shall confer with our consultant, Roberta Clerk, to adjust these figures accordingly.

9. Your firm shall be liable for any injury or damage to persons or property caused by your negligent acts during the pick up of paper at XYZ Company and you shall maintain adequate insurance coverage for this risk.

10. The term of this agreement shall stand subject to the right of XYZ Company to terminate it at any time upon one month's notice.

11. Please return a signed a copy of this agreement along with a signed and notarized Guarantee of Destruction Affidavit to:

    Carl Brown, Chief Financial Officer
    XYZ Company
    987 Johnson Road
    Anytown, MI 12345

If the aforesaid terms of our agreement are acceptable, please indicate your assent in the space provided below. We anticipate a long and mutually rewarding relationship with your firm.

By: _____

Title: _____

Date: _____

By: _____

Title: _____

Date: _____

Exhibit G.2   (cont.)

Appendix G (cont.)

Newspaper Contract Between
ABC Industries and Community Recycling Center

1. ABC Industries of Bloomington, Indiana agrees to accept newspaper from Community Recycling Center hereafter referred to as "CRC" of Champaign, Illinois.

2. CRC agrees to meet the allowable contamination levels set by ABC. The newspaper shall be dry and anything that comes in the newspaper can be recycled with the paper. The newspaper can be left bundled and bagged. However, if outthrows (e.g., kraft bags, cardboard boxes, and paper other than what comes in the newspaper) exceeds 5 percent then that amount in excess of 5 percent shall not be paid for. In addition, ABC can dock payment for a load of newspaper or reject it for being wet.

3. Newspaper can be shipped loose or baled to ABC.

4. ABC will supply a trailer in well-maintained condition for storage of either loose or baled newspaper. A minimum of 35,000 pounds is needed for free shipping by ABC-supplied trailers. No minimum quantity and no shipping charge shall be assigned to trailers that are pulled at ABC's request.

5. For the period January 1, 1992 through December 31, 1992, ABC will purchase all the newspaper volume CRC generates within this period up to a maximum of 700 tons. Additional tonnage can be shipped and the period of shipment can be extended past December 31, 1992 upon mutual agreement by ABC and CRC.

6. All baled newspaper shall be purchased at the highest price listed for No. 1 newspaper-Chicago market by the Official Board Market (312-938-2300) at the time the newspaper is shipped. All loose newspaper shall be purchased at a price that is $10 per ton below the highest price listed for No. 1 newspaper-Chicago market by the Official Board Market at the time the newspaper is shipped.

7. However, notwithstanding the market price listed by the Official Board Market, in no case shall the price for loose newspaper be lower than $30 per ton during the term of this contract outlined in Section 5. Also, if the price paid to the Center exceeds $50 per ton the difference shall be divided evenly between the parties.

8. ABC will provide a monthly report which states the guaranteed price for the waste for that month and showing year-to-date and monthly totals by waste grade.

Exhibit G.3   Example Newspaper Recycling Contract (USEPA, 1991a)

Appendix G (cont.)

Page 2

9. Payment for all loads of newspaper received by ABC shall be paid for within 30 days. In the event payment is not received on a timely basis, CRC shall give written notice that said payment was not received. ABC shall remit payment within five (5) days of receiving this written notice. If payment is not made within five (5) days, a penalty interest shall accrue at the rate of twelve percent (12%) per annum from the date payment was due. In addition, CRC shall have the right upon such default to take court action for payment and/or to cancel this contract.

10. Any rejection of newspaper shall require notification of the Director or Operations Manager of the Community Recycling Center (217-351-4495) so that they have the right to remove and resell the newspaper. Any newspaper used by ABC from a rejected load shall be paid for at the regular price.

11. The term of this agreement shall stand subject to the right of Community Recycling Center to terminate it at any time upon one month's notice.

12. The term of this contract shall commence on January 1, 1992 and end on December 31, 1992.

ABC: _____

Title: _____

Date: _____

Community Recycling Center: _____

Title: _____

Date: _____

Exhibit G.3   (cont.)

References

ASTM Committee D34.01.02, Waste Sampling. <u>Method for Determination of the Composition of Unprocessed Municipal Solid Waste (DRAFT)</u>

Becker, J., Noble, G., Richards, A., and Vasseur, L. 1988. <u>West Cook County [Illinois] Solid Waste Needs Assessment</u> Prepared for Northeastern Illinois Planning Commission and West Central Municipal Conference. Chicago, IL.

BFI (Browning Ferris Industries). 1987. <u>The Possibilities & Practicalities of Business Waste Recycling</u> Developed for Mecklenburg County, NC.

Burstein, D. 1990. "Environmental Engineering," pp. 1.1-1.94 in <u>Standard Handbook of Environmental Engineering</u> R. Corbitt, Editor. McGraw-Hill, Inc., New York, NY.

Carruth, D., and Klee, A. 1969. <u>Analysis of Solid Waste Composition. Statistical Technique to Determine Sample Size</u> (SW-19ts) U.S. Dept. of Health and Human Welfare Bureau of Solid Waste Management. NTIS Publication PB-216 584. Cincinnati, OH.

Casey, C. Waste Management Coordinator, University of Iowa. 1991. Personal Communication. Iowa City, IA.

Ching, R. Recycling Coordinator, Rutgers University. 1991. Personal Communication.

Chiu, Y., Eyster, J., and Gipe, G. 1976. Solid Waste Generation Rates of a University Community. <u>ASCE Journal of Environmental Engineering</u> 102(6):1285-1289.

DC (Dartmouth College). 1988. <u>Reduce, Recycle and Educate: A Solid Waste Management Program for Dartmouth College</u> Hanover, NH.

Franks, G. Recycling Coordinator, N.C. State University at Raleigh. 1991. Personal communication. Raleigh, NC.

Getz, R. Assoc. Dir. Physical Plant Admin., University of Illinois at Chicago. 1991. Personal Communication.

Glysson, E. 1990. "Solid Waste," pp. 8.1-8.193 in <u>Standard Handbook of Environmental Engineering</u> R. Corbitt, Editor. McGraw-Hill, Inc., New York, NY

Hargett, T. and Osborn, R. 1989. "Cornell Recycles: A Major University Commitment" <u>Facilities Manager</u> Summer Issue, pp. 40-47.

Hoss, T. Recycling Coordinator, University of Illinois-Urbana/Champaign. 1991. Personal Communication.

ILCMS (Illinois Dept. Central Management Services). <u>Printing Contract Sealed Bid Proof, FY 92 (No. X0313)</u> Springfield, IL.

Marks, J. 1990. "Recycling Program Development at the University of Michigan" Presentation at the Michigan Recycling Coalition Annual Conference, October 3, 1990. Ann Arbor, MI

Marks, J. Recycling Coordinator, University of Michigan. 1991. Personal Communication.

May, C. Recycling Coordinator, Yale University. 1989. *Paper at Yale: A Solid Waste Management Strategy for Purchasing, Use and Collection Under Connecticut's Recycling Law* School of Forestry and Environmental Studies, Yale University. New Haven, CT.

NU (Northwestern University). 1990. *Recycling Task Force Report* Evanston, IL

Potter, J. 1990. *Solid Waste Recycling - A Proposal for Texas A&M University* Master's Thesis. College Station, TX.

Rushbrook, P., and Ball, R. 1988. "Improved Estimation of Waste Arisings Using Limited Sample Sizes" *Waste Management & Research* 6(1):35-44

Savage, G. Cal Recovery Systems, Hercules, CA. 1991. Personal Communication regarding waste composition at University of California at Berkley.

Skomra, M. 1989. "Dartmouth Recycles: Is it the Solution to Waste Disposal Problems ?" *Executive Housekeeping Today* January, 1989 pp. 5-6.

Smithers, W. Solid Waste Manager, Cornell University. 1991. Personal Communication. Ithaca, NY

UBC (University of British Columbia). 1991. *Building a Sustainable Community: An Integrated Solid Waste Management Programme Planning Element* Prepared by Resource Integration Systems, Ltd. for UBC. Vancouver, BC, Canada.

UCLA (University of California-Los Angeles) 1991. *UCLA Recycling Program* Facilities Management Office. Los Angeles, CA.

UIUC (University of Illinois at Urbana - Champaign). 1989. *Campus-Wide Recycling Program Report and Recommendations to the Vice Chancellor for Administrative Affairs* Prepared by Recycling Task Force. Urbana, IL.

UIUC. 1990. *Annual Recycling and Materials Reduction Report* Urbana, IL.

UIUC. 1991. *Annual Recycling and Materials Reduction Report* Urbana, IL.

UMAA (University of Michigan at Ann Arbor). No Date. Getting Started - *A Recycling Kit for the Office at the University of Michigan Office Paper Recycling Program* Plant Grounds and Waste Management Department. Ann Arbor, MI.

UMAA. 1989. *Integrated Solid Waste Management for UM Housing Final Report and Recommendations* Housing division and Plant Department Solid Waste Management Task Force. Ann Arbor, MI

UMAA. 1991. *Fiscal year 1991 Recycling Volumes* University of Michigan Plant Grounds and Waste Management Department. Ann Arbor, MI.

UMMS (University of Minnesota at Minneapolis-St. Paul). 1990. *The University of Minnesota Recycling Program Implementation and Operation Manual* University of Minnesota Department of Physical Plant Operations. Minneapolis, MN.

USEPA 1990a. *Characterization of MSW in the U.S.: 1990 Update* Publication USEAP/530-SW/90-042A. Washington, D.C.

USEPA 1990b. Developing a Comprehensive Federal Office Recycling Program: A Handbook. Washington, DC

USEPA. 1991a. Closing the Loop: Purchasing Recycled Paper: A Guide for Purchasing Officials Prepared by A.T. Kearny and E.H. Pechan & Associates for EPA Region 5 and the Great Lakes Region Waste Paper Work Group. EPA/905/9-81/014.

USEPA. 1991b. Marketing Waste Paper: A Recycling Coordinator's Handbook Prepared by Franklin Associates for EPA Region 5 and the Great Lakes Region Waste Paper Work Group. EPA/905/9-81/015

UW (University of Washington). 1989. University of Washington Waste Stream Analysis Phase 1: Solid Waste Minimization and Management Study Prepared by CCA Inc. Seattle, WA.

UWP (University of Wisconsin-Parkside). 1990. Final Report Office Paper Recycling Program at University of Wisconsin-Parkside. Wisconsin Energy Bureau, Waste-to-Energy & Recycling Program Project Report (Grant Program Contract ADI 89041). Madison, WI.

Additional Sources of Information

General

A Study to Develop a Predictive Technique for the Estimation of Collectible Solid Waste in the United States Prepared by Franklin Associates, Ltd. for Argonne National Laboratory. NTIS ANL/CNSV-TM-171. 1985.

"An Up Close Look at Office Waste" Cesar, M. Resource Recycling 10(6):63-66. June, 1991.

"Colleges Upgrade Recycling Efforts" Biocycle 31(2):68-71. February, 1990.

Earth Print: Environmentally Conscious Printing for the 90's Doff, K., Lawrence, J., Staley, S. Holladay-Tyler Printing Corp. Glenn Dale, MD. 1990.

Evaluation of Institutional Arrangements for Solid Waste Recycling Hostetler, R. Prepared for National Science Foundation by University of Wisconsin Institute for Environmental Studies. NTIS PB-247 234. 1975.

53 Simple Things Universities and Colleges Can Do to Reduce Waste: Case Studies of University Source Reduction, Recycling, and Composting Prepared for California Integrated Solid Waste Management Office by Resource Integration Systems, Ltd. Portland, OR. 1991.

Office Paper Recycling: An Implementation Manual USEPA Office of Solid Waste Management. EPA/530-SW-90-001. Washington, D.C. 1990.

"Reclaiming Wastes From Business and Industry" Walsh, P., and O'Leary, P. Waste Age 19(8):157-162. August, 1988.

Recycling: A Planning Guide for Communities New York State Department of Environmental Conservation Division of Solid Waste. Albany, NY. 1989.

Recycling at University Campuses Liebert, R. Prepared for University of Illinois at Urbana-Champaign by Survey Research Laboratory. Urbana, IL. 1988.

"Recycling Goes to College" Watson, T. Resource Recycling 9(4):76-81. April, 1990.

The Environmentally Friendly Office: Recycling Paper and Other Items in Your Office Greater Chicago Recycling Industry Council. Chicago, IL. 1990.

"University Thinkers Design Own Do-it-Yourself PS Collection" Recycling Polystyrene 2(1):1-2. January, 1991.

U.S. Postal Service Recycling Guide Handbook AS-550. Washington, D.C. 1991.

Wisconsin State Agency Recycling Guidance Manual Wisconsin Department of Administration. Madison, WI. 1991.

Food Waste

"Separate Collection of Biowaste" Krogmann, U. Proceedings of the Global Pollution Prevention Conference Washington, D.C. 1991.

"Food Waste Composting: Institutions Get a Taste" Watson, T. Resource Recycling 9(11):45-47. November, 1990.

"Restaurants Recycle" Westerman, M. Resource Recycling 10(1):78-83. January, 1991.

Hazardous Waste

Guides to Pollution Prevention: Research and Educational Institutions USEPA Risk Reduction Engineering Laboratory. EPA/625/7-90/010. Cincinnati, OH. 1990.

Hazardous Waste Management in Institutions and Colleges Lenox Institute for Research, Inc. NTIS PB86-194180. Lenox, MA. 1985.

Waste Disposal in Academic Institutions Kaufman, J. Lewis Publishers, Chelsea, MI. 1990.

Hospitals

Developing a Recycling Program: A Guide for Hospitals New Jersey Hospital Association Council on Management Practices. 1991.

Guides to Pollution Prevention: Selected Hospital Waste Streams USEPA Risk Reduction Research Laboratory. EPA/625/7-90/009. Cincinnati, OH. 1990.

"Hospital Waste Management" Cheremisinoff, P., and Shah, M. Pollution Engineering (4):60-66. April, 1990.

"Waste Reduction and Recycling at Hospitals: Building a Healthy Community" Nelson, M., and Steinberger, M. Resource Recycling 9(11):32-38. November, 1990.